BYOUNG CHO · BCHO PARTNERS

IMAGINING

The Choreography of Land and Architecture

CONTENTS

9	Introduction
14	Interview with the BCHO Partners
38	Joongangchung Museum
52	CGV Warehouse Renovation
70	Hyundai Motors GBC
90	Buddhist Cultural Center and Dormitory
112	Milan Expo—World Crisis
126	Louis Vuitton Maison Seoul
144	Greenscape Libya
166	Dana Point Hotel
180	Sampyo Headquarters
194	Visang Headquarters
214	Seun District #4
230	Gana Art Center and Villas
248	Los Angeles Communal Housing
262	Pyeongchang Winter Olympics Stadium
276	Young Hak Lee Sculpture Museum
288	Pillye Village, Seorak Mountain
300	AYU25 Botanical Café
314	Neutra House—Studio Addition
326	Ahn Choong-kun Memorial Library
334	416 Memorial Park and Museum
350	Hongcheon Hotel
358	Bandong-ri Prefab House
370	Four Piece Housing
382	Seomi Furniture Gallery
392	BCHO Partners
394	Partner Profiles
396	BCHO Staff

INTRODUCTION

by Byoung Cho (Founder)

I believe the unbuilt projects exhibited here reflect our (BCHO Partners) ideas as much as the built ones do. In some aspects, they show the concept more clearly than built ones. Through the process of finalizing the design and construction, the clarity of the concept gets lost in the midst of the various influences such as budget, clients' understanding, city review boards' opinion, and so forth.

We get critiques and reviews of our design always based on our built projects through publications, exhibitions, or forums. But unbuilt projects disappear from our sight and memories rather quickly. Once in a while I go down into the basement of our office building where we have the firm's archive and sit down with the black binders trying to check whether all the documents are organized in the right place. I enjoy finding old drawings that initiated the design of buildings we have already built. Sometimes I find myself surprised to notice while looking at drawings or unbuilt projects that these often look very similar to our current projects.

Unbuilt projects, built buildings, sketches, and idea notes are probably all on one palette in my mind. They exist intermingled in the deep ocean of my subconsciousness floating above the surface when they are needed—sometimes without known reason or logic. I sometimes wonder, "what if the unbuilt and abandoned ones had been built?" Some unbuilt projects are quickly forgotten with the passage of time, while some keep returning back to my mind when I rest, walk, or meditate.

The choreography of land and architecture

Throughout the projects over the last thirty years, I find one consistent interest, which is a concern for the land. Personally, the term "land" speaks of a latent field of existing conditions—conditions of topography, nature, history, memories, and culture found in a given site. It is not so much the introduction of new forms, but the choreography of these site forces into an experienced and perceivable whole or scenery (hence comes the term, "land architecture") that defines our practice and role as architects. The interest for the relationship of the built works to the condition of the land—in other words, the excavation, activation, and weaving of the site elements into life—compels us to work extensively through site plans and site sections. Formal expressions come last, probably with the least amount of interest, or at times, left intentionally unexpressed.

Even from my very early projects in the cities of Lugano, Boston, and Montreal, one can easily find that I have had a strong interest in making something out of the existing site conditions. All three projects find potential from the existing site conditions and seek to solve problematic issues with minimum introduction of new structures. The final proposals appear void of formal gestures as the key operations performed on each site are literal acts of "emptying," "cutting," and "connecting." The surgical procedures of these projects are each compelled by tangible and practical diagnoses to restore the land into an organic entity. Emptying volumes from the massive concrete building of the Boston State Service Center to reintroduce a flow of public movement, air, and sunlight into the depths of a dilapidated area, or the cutting away of existing structures from the abandoned port of

Montreal to reveal the layers of time and history to the public are driven by the motive to create an organic land architecture, in which the multiple elements of past, present, and future may coexist.

The collection of projects that follows in the subsequent chapters reflects the breadth of our past explorations in the relationship between the land and architecture. One can easily discover that our strategy for an urban site, such as the Seomi Furniture Gallery or Seun District #4, departs substantially from architectural solutions that address a site in nature, as in our African coastal project: Greenscape Libya. In section, a specific ground condition may call for the need to insert a volume underground, while the very same volume in a different site may compel us to lift the volume aboveground (much like the Hyundai Motors GBC). For certain projects, the addressing of the land condition appears more evidently in plan. The linearity found in the projects Woori Village, the Village of Dancing Fish, and Southcape Linear Hotel, for example, are born from practical attempts to define spaces while building harmoniously into the existing topography. Material applications also trace back to site-specific contexts as in the solar control screens of the Buddhist Cultural Center and Dormitory in Houston. As such, this monograph presents an invaluable opportunity for us to revisit our collection of unbuilt projects through the common lens of the land. While the architectural language may vary, the conceptual seeds that formulate each project all trace back to our interpretation of the given land condition and capture our very attempt toward defining and creating "land architecture."

Seoul, 2021

INTERVIEW WITH THE BCHO PARTNERS

by Associate Professor Leif Høgfeldt Hansen, April 2021

BCHO Partners: Byoung Cho (Founder), Ji-hyun Lee, Ja-yoon Yoon, Kyung-jin Hong, Yerie Kim (former Project Architect)

The beginning of the BCHO Partners office

Is it possible to explain how the BCHO Partners office started and its early approach to different architectural assignments?

Byoung: The office started up with a couple of small projects. Those projects were located in a squatter area, which is similar to a slum in Western countries, where poor people, after the Korean War, moved and settled down on a hillside without the legal right of the land. It was a dense area divided into small building lots, where many families lived together. Through more planned urbanization, the government tried to establish service roads for fire safety, forcing the demolition of buildings along the new service roads for fire engine access. Many building lots—and even houses—were cut into halves during the process. Our first project was in such a place.

In South Korea, we have a law for a small building to be a minimum of 484 square feet (45 square meters). Our first project was even smaller than that. We built a tiny house for three different families on a 484-square-foot (45-square-meter) plot. With this project, we learned quickly about Korean society, people living in low-class homes, and unskilled construction workers and their mindsets and reactions on a building site. It was disappointing to experience that the construction

BCHO Forum, 2020, Concrete Box House		Conversation with BCHO Partners, 2021

team didn't want to listen to the architect or look at drawings. There were always excuses that ended up in economic disputes. That is why we started handling the building process ourselves on every building we designed. The office began with designing small practical buildings. In our early projects, we learned about the constructions and how to control them, so already there, we could experiment with exciting details. In the end, we produced more interesting buildings. However, we did not do competitions or try out unique projects because we were working with ordinary middle-class people's projects. We tried to be inventive with construction and detailing and to find ways to make compromises to realize the buildings. Because of this practical approach, our projects did not start with experimental, conceptual ideas. We focused on using constructions and materials and the working process with third parties or other people on a building site. If you understand their approach, it is possible to communicate much better. Creating positive experiences for all parties involved makes the building process much faster and more efficient.

Until 1999 I was in charge of architectural design and my brother assisted me with the construction process. That year I was invited to teach in the United States, so I realized that I could not be responsible for all of it, and the company was divided into two separate parts. My brother was in charge of architectural construction, and I was doing architectural design.

How did later assignments and projects develop after the office got more established?

Byoung: Gradually, assignments with higher budgets came to the office, and we obtained projects with better conditions. However, sometimes these projects had less room for experiments and few opportunities to take risks in the design process. It looked like those projects with more money and

Four-box house   Three-box house   U-shaped house

complicated programs tended to produce more rigid solutions. We finished the Village of the Dancing Fish project and similar buildings during the first ten years. Most of our projects at that time were built, and we did not do any competitions. Then we started to be invited to developer projects and invited competitions. Especially in the invited competitions, it was possible to test other concepts and ideas and develop them into design proposals.

Our architectural design is also inspired by Korean culture. In the beginning, we investigated variations of the traditional Korean building typologies developed from the shape of a simple box: I-shapes, L-shapes, U-shapes and ▫-shapes. BCHO Partners started to use other typologies with the Twin Trees building in 2010 with a plan layout generated out of the organic footprint from the existing road system near Gyeongbokgung Palace in Seoul.

It is essential to point out that the underlining idea in all our projects, besides construction, materials, and budget control, is to care about the given conditions, especially the land's given condition. Architects typically call it the site, but this word also involves more social and legal aspects. In my understanding, land is more a topographical thing that can also include the surrounding buildings and landscape. It will be descriptive to call the built architecture designed by BCHO Partners as "land architecture." One can find these in our current rather large-scale projects, such as the Seonneung Terrace Hotel or the Seed Project.

How do the younger partners experience current South Korean architecture and the BCHO office's work from an international perspective?

Ji-hyun: From an international perspective, I think the quality of contemporary South Korean architecture is relatively low. This lack of quality probably comes from the fact that the infrastructure to make good buildings is not yet well cultivated compared to most other occidental countries.

I believe that clients must commission their works to architects with total confidence. Architects must be entrusted with complete responsibility and be allowed some financial flexibility. At the same time, better engineering quality and mature construction culture should also be guaranteed.

After having gone through a devastating war in the 1950s and a reconstruction phase for another half a century, South Korea has reached its current economic and social status with such rapid speed. But architecture always begins from the given condition—it builds upon the given environment, given budget, given construction technology and workers, and given clients.

At the beginning of Byoung's career, he made small-sized buildings with interesting details with unskilled labor and extremely low budget. He was focused on finding the best solution out of what was readily available. I believe that such pursuits can lead to another level of creativity and authenticity in Korea's contemporary architectural scene.

Yerie: South Korea's progress in development after the Korean War has been significant. However, we cannot help but admit that most South Korean developers have been more interested in profitability than softer cultural values. During the last few decades, the speed of development took precedence over the pursuit of architectural quality.

South Korean architects have had little opportunity to learn from or even participate in international contexts. Accordingly, international architects have had minimal information on the development of Korean architecture. At the same time, the younger generation of South Korean architects is responding to their seniors' situation with skepticism and have started to display their interpretation and ideas on South Korean architecture. It is as if a suppressed yearning of the younger generation has begun to burst out.

Byoung Cho's situation is different. At a relatively early stage, he had a chance to study architecture abroad. He didn't stay still only to receive and reflect on the international architecture. He was proactive and developed his own personal style and perspective on architecture, which successfully integrated his innate regionalism with an international style. Now his architecture sets a good precedent for young architects in South Korea who have begun to build their own architectural perspectives.

Southcape Linear Hotel

Southcape Linear Hotel

Jipyoung Guesthouse

BCHO Partners today

How do you, as partners at BCHO Partners, consider the recurring qualities of the work designed today?

Ja-yoon: BCHO's approach seems to be considerably influenced by Eastern architecture. Buildings are closely linked to the land or existing site conditions and have a high consideration of a natural interface or flow between interior and exterior spaces. One can see this not only in our early small projects, but also in our current large-scale works such as the Seonneung Terrace Hotel and the Seed Project. Another feature is the pursuit of harmony and empirical quality in simple structures. Rather than concentrating on architectural theories, the office attempts to make practical architectural aspects such as construction, ventilation, and daylighting into positive experiences.

BCHO Partners considers the relationship with the site as essential and emphasizes the site's empirical and natural aspects rather than the building itself. Architecture built in places with an excellent natural environment, such as Jipyoung Guesthouse or Southcape Linear Hotel, was adapted according to each site's appearance or natural environmental characteristics, creating a complex layout and design integrated with nature. Similar approaches can be studied among the unbuilt projects, for instance, the Dana Point Hotel; the Pillye Village, Seorak Mountain; and the Ahn Choong-kun Memorial Library.

Projects proposed in urban contexts, such as the Hyundai Motors GBC project and the Seun District #4 proposal, were intended to create nature-friendly places and secure a positive public character by proposing buildings on top of a new park or landscape. BCHO's work aims to find a unique design solution according to the site contexts. The pursuit of harmony characterizes it by considering the organic relationship between the surrounding environment and the building.

Ji-hyun: In BCHO's works, there have always been attempts to search for specific Korean aesthetic qualities. As described in some of Byoung Cho's recent essays, "the Korean concept of *mahk* is defined as having a status of being imperfect and rough, but appropriately rough." It often appears that a natural occurrence or incident during a process is used to design a spontaneous architectural purpose, treating the building as part of nature. This aspect is related to how BCHO deals with the land. The process of trying to adapt to the site contours either in contrast to or in correspondence with the land is part of the initial design. The legacy of "adapting to nature" is a regional aspect that has always been the case for traditional Korean architecture.

In terms of forms, BCHO's work pursues simple, honest, and functional shapes that properly accommodate their purpose, rather than playing with shapes for their own sake. In addition to that, the materials are displayed in an authentic way—especially concrete and wood.

Yerie: A recurring feature in BCHO's architecture is the use of an elevated plateau, or new ground. You can find this feature in most projects, whether built or unbuilt, and whether situated in nature or urban contexts. This gesture obtains different purposes, but the most dominant reason is establishing a relationship with the surroundings. In some projects, this elevated plateau becomes an extension of the natural ground into the architecture. On the other hand, this new plateau functions as a buffer in the conflict between the existing and the new, harmonizing two distinct conditions.

Recently in Korea, many architects have started to focus on recycling old buildings, and BCHO Partners seems to agree with this trend for sustainability. Since South Korea is now far past the development phase following the Korean War, the remaining undeniable challenge for Korean architects lies in utilizing old architecture. BCHO focuses on upcycling rather than recycling old architecture with a humble and straightforward approach. Instead of demolishing the old, BCHO tries to save the old structure, add on a few excellent harmonizing ideas—and at other times be in contrast to the old. This creative approach brings a fresh vitality to the old architecture.

Do you think it is possible to detect a specific working process at BCHO Partners?

Kyung-jin: One distinctive characteristic that makes BCHO Partners different from other design offices is its constant interest in materiality. Furthermore, this has quite an effect on our working process as well. As material should be imagined in its actual scale and also in regards to its constructability, BCHO Partners investigates details from a very early stage. As the office pursues the design further in the process, there are considerable variations and options, which results in a final proposal that may be different from the initial ideas and drawings. In this regard, the fact that we

Hyundai Training Center

Seo-Bo Park Residence

F1963 Kiswire Factory

study multiple details from the early stage can be inefficient. However, this method has been a fruitful process in the office so far because it naturally leads to similar design attempts in the following projects and evolves into new projects in the same "family." The aluminum façade series we tried out in our recent projects, such as the Hyundai Training Center, Seo-Bo Park Residence, and F1963 Kiswire Factory, seems to be a good example. What we studied and learned from the previous built project keeps evolving and affects the following projects.

Another working process we emphasize is site supervision. When we design buildings based on multiple materials, no matter how detailed the drawings are, there is always a difference between the drawings and the reality on the construction site. An exciting thing to learn from Byoung is not to be agitated by situations that require design changes and improvisation on-site. On the contrary, he seems to embrace alterations and redesigns for new site conditions. The receptive attitude toward reality is related to the Korean aesthetic characteristic called *mahk*, which Ji-hyun brought up in her previous talk on the recurring qualities of the BCHO office. I think the quality of receptiveness and improvisation will be hard to experience in the drawings of the unbuilt projects in this book. If it could be expressed, it would be fascinating. Many unbuilt projects in this book show our clear design idea because they do not involve practical restraints. Yet, it may not be easy to fully deliver our deep engagement with reality in our working processes to the readers.

I have noticed that projects are developed with multiple schemes or prototypes tested during the design phase. Is that correct?

Yerie: I worked on the Sampyo Headquarters project in Seoul and the Buddhist Cultural Center and Dormitory project in Houston, Texas, and a private project in Los Angeles. These projects are different but have a similar method. In the Sampyo project, a small group of architects also developed several schemes.

At the first presentation, a few schemes were chosen. Then these schemes were developed further for a new presentation, and this system went on again and again. As a project designer, one may feel that it is a waste of time—but it is part of a development process. Furthermore, it can also be a development process for young architects' growth. Discussions about several different schemes among the designers, from juniors to seniors, allow junior designers to be involved in the project with more passion and subjective consciousness. Rather than simply watching the overall process, in BCHO Partners, young architects have opportunities to participate in the project with his or her scheme.

When we develop multiple schemes, we try to foresee the pros and cons of each scheme, possible details we can achieve in the given budget, and other realistic conditions. Even though these considerations are not included in the early-stage presentation, selected alternatives are the results of the discussion covering general ideas and detailed aspects of the project.

For a smaller project for a private client, the working process was slightly different. The design team developed a few schemes at the beginning. Once a promising scheme was chosen, the design development process started being narrowed down faster than on bigger projects. Several design alternatives had been developed, but they stayed at the idea level and would flourish the general selected design concept.

Ji-hyun: In the Seed Project, the office explored as many options as possible, regarding the land and sustainability. We started this project with a care for true sustainability especially since the project was to be on a landfill site.

Model studies for the Seed Project

Unbuilt projects

Let us now focus on some of the unbuilt projects displayed in this book. Your CGV Warehouse renovation project in Incheon City's port was on its way for a long time. Is it possible to explain more about the work?

Ja-yoon: The CGV Warehouse renovation was part of the Incheon City Urban Regeneration Project to secure urban publicity and provide a cultural complex for citizens by renovating an unused grain warehouse located at the eighth pier adjacent to the old city center. The existing steel-frame constructed warehouse was built in the 1980s and is one of the most significant warehouse buildings without interior columns in Asia. It was a project that Incheon City led, and was carried out by CGV (Domestic Film Business), a private developer, to operate movies, culture, accommodation, and commercial facilities for twenty years.

CGV wanted to include various programs, such as cafés, restaurants, movie theaters, entertainment facilities, public parks, and start-up support facilities. The requirement from the local government was that 30 percent of the programs should involve the citizens. The diverse and complex requirements were integrated into a flow by creating a new landscape with a sloped platform inside the warehouse.

We proposed creating a green axis that went through the middle of the long 3,9823-foot-by-484-foot (370-meter-by-45-meter) warehouse and opened up through a transparent glass roof to connect to the city and the port. A platform or "new terrain" was proposed to rise along the inside of the warehouse to capture various private and public programs in the large building while enhancing the spatial scale and experience in the existing large and open warehouse. The platform's upper part was proposed as an open plan that makes a visual connection from one end to the other. The large warehouse's dramatic height and space were experienced and emphasized even more by the platform's movement up and down.

The facility system and the floor plan were flexibly planned to respond to changes in programs during operation through the years. Special programs that had to be noise-blocked and compartmentalized were placed under the platform and functionally separated. Different movie theaters were integrated into the plan to emphasize the connection to the CGV company.

The project's design lasted nearly one-and-a-half years from the bidding to the later stages of the construction documents. During that period, the client's corporate finances deteriorated. It was calculated that the project did not produce enough business feasibility compared to investment costs, so they gave up the project. Unfortunately, the project was cancelled at the last stage of the design, while it was undergoing countless consultations and building permits with various private and public sectors.

I think the design success of this project lies in creating an open, accessible public space on an urban scale and developing the port's connection strategy to the old city. The open space in the interior with flexible programs in this huge and long warehouse would have been extremely pleasant. It would have created an exciting and unique area as a new type of public cultural space connected to the cinema.

Another interesting new project with a unique site condition is the Seonneung Terrace Hotel and Housing project in Seoul. How is this developing?

Kyung-jin: The Seonneung Terrace Hotel and Housing project is still in the design development phase. When we first started this project, we only had the commission to design the façade. In the original scheme, the building volume was placed in the shape of an "L." In this first proposal, the outdoor garden was connected to the Seongjeongneung Royal Tomb, a World Heritage Site in a natural setting, but with no strong relationship to the interior space. However, we wanted to invite nature deep into the interior space. We thought it would be more appropriate to have an atrium in the middle of the interior and bring nature into the building, so we proposed this new scheme, which was appreciated and started the whole project.

The project's main idea is to link the building to the Seonjeongneung Royal Tomb on the south side of the building. To maximize the benefit of the site, having a cultural heritage in a green setting versus the hub of the business district, we set two main entrances, one to the hotel's lobby to the south, and prioritized the connection with Seonjeongneung and the other to the commercial lobby

Seonneung Terrace Hotel and Housing, 2020

to the north and increased convenience to the public. This location can also be explained with the term "ground-scape." On the north side of the building is "urbanscape" connecting to the city, and on the south side is "landscape," connecting to the green nature. In contrast to other high-rise buildings with platforms as landscape buffer zones designed by BCHO Partners, this project allows the landscape of the royal tomb area to flow directly into the building by emptying the south ground floor inside the building.

The project had to have multiple programs to distribute business risks, such as hotels, apartments, and studios. Under this circumstance and to comply with the height regulations under the Cultural Heritage Management Act, a steel Vierendeel truss structural system became an intelligent solution to obtain as many open floors as possible. This space optimization increases the profitability of the project. At the same time, it achieves the concept of one large open space without columns for the lobby and a great visual connection to the landscape. The office worked with a creative structural engineer, King-le Chang, who did an excellent job to achieve the benefits of this construction system. I think the integration between the engineers and architects strengthened the qualities of the project.

Is it possible to explain the ideas behind another recent project for the Visang Headquarters?

Ji-hyun: Visang Headquarters is being built, and work started in July 2021. However, we categorized it as an unbuilt project because the client did not select the design themes we wanted to realize due to budget and its purpose.

During the process, the project had three primary schemes.

1. The overall city seemed quite sterile, so we have decided to make the concept of a central courtyard, forming a city within a city, by making the building mass in a "□" shape.

2. The second scheme was making the podium part distinctively approachable so that there is a long circular ramp connecting from the ground floor to the first floor. And the rest of the office space is planned as open plan, universal.

3. The other scheme was to break the masses into pieces, so small-scaled alleys and squares would be formed within one building. We thought it was essential to make specific city-scale contexts within the office.

  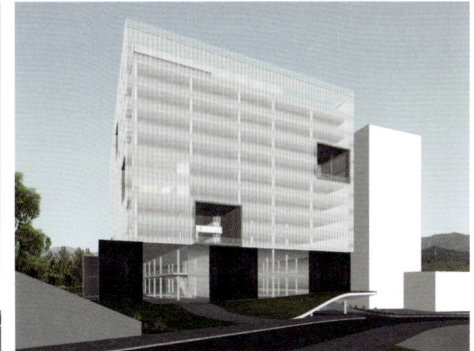

Early design schemes for Visang Headquarters

All of these schemes were attempts to make the building more publicly approachable.

In the first scheme, we made the office building mass float above the ground, obtaining a distinctive "ground-scape" quality, and the mass itself would gain more urban character. But, this idea was eventually abandoned because of budget constraints; once it forms a ▫-shape, the building envelope area increases more than twice, which meant a considerable increase in cost.

In the third scheme, by dividing one large mass into three or four smaller masses, the workspace is contained in those separated volumes, and the public spaces are placed in the small-scaled alleys and squares, forming both large- and small-scale contrasts. However, this approach was also excluded, as the space became too fragmented for use. In the end, it was appropriate to make a generic, universal, and flexible working space within a minimal budget.

In architecture, there are always compromises with reality and constraints. And the very balance between realistic solutions with compromises and creativity is always critical. The final Visang Headquarters scheme, currently being built, does not have the degree of spatial complexity that we initially pursued. However, we are satisfied with the result that we achieved in the end.

BCHO partners has recently been designing a Buddhist Cultural Center in Texas for multiple clients. How did this project go?

Yerie: The Buddhist Cultural Center and Dormitory client was a Buddhist religious organization with its roots in East Asia. The organization believed the Buddhist Cultural Center in Houston could be a centripetal focus of the religion in the United States. They wanted to have a new temple with educational and administrative facilities in one building. They also wanted to have a dormitory for the monks and visitors, with a possibility of a later expansion.

The design team started the project by visiting the site in Texas. We read recommended books written by their most famous and respected monk and participated in their weekly ceremony to thoroughly understand their religion. After studying their religion and experiencing the regional architecture and climate, we could initiate our design.

The design intended to make a modern temple that could embrace young generations and multiple races and be in contrast to a previously poorly designed temple placed right in front of our potential building location. The dormitory design had many folds to reflect the demand from the client of a possible future expansion. We considered the circulation between the three buildings on the site—the existing temple, the new cultural center, and the dormitory. Because of the unbearable and harsh sunlight during summer in Texas, it is almost impossible to move without shade between buildings if distances are far.

The cultural center consists of three masses of different programs and has a small courtyard in between. This courtyard becomes a detached, purified, and serene ground protected from the vast land outside.

We considered Houston's climate and the client's central concern of flooding as the most critical issue regarding landscape design. In order to make a beautiful landscape design into reality, it is vital to be responsive to climate. We placed ditches along the site perimeter and a collecting water reservoir to avoid flooding, which occurs severely once every few years in the region. We elevated both buildings from the ground. This elevation of the building resulted in a grand entrance stair from the courtyard to the cultural center with a semi-open corridor with repeated louvers, which led visitors and monks from outer lands to sacred space.

The client was a branch of Buddhism that initially started in East Asia, which in reality made our client be two parties, one in the United States and one in Asia. The people in Houston provided the project to us with a great expectation of their religion to blossom in the harsh land. The client in Houston was very satisfied with our design and eager to proceed further on this project. However, the administrative organization in the main temple declined the project after deep consideration, and the local Houston branch could not change that decision.

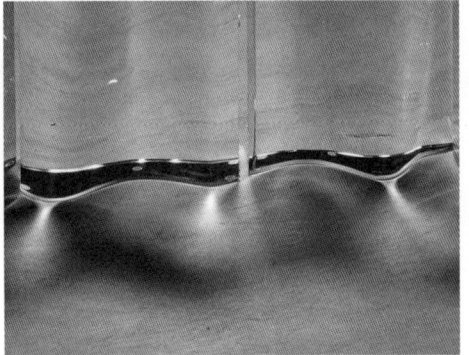

Façade studies for Louis Vuitton Maison Seoul (glass, 3D print)

In the Louis Vuitton flagship store competition, the office experimented with a dominant undulated glass façade. Was this an intention to connect the interior to the surroundings?

Byoung: In some of our urban competitions, it might be slightly different with the connection to the surrounding land. For example, the Louis Vuitton flagship store project was located in an urban area, where the landscape is rigid because other buildings have occupied every inch of the land. The program, on the other hand, was a vital aspect. The Louis Vuitton building was supposed to be an important flagship store for fashion shopping. It should have characteristic design features and be very recognizable on Seoul's most fancy shopping streets. The office tried to experiment with the concept of the shopping experience. We used the material glass for one prominent undulated façade, which distorted the inside's image when the people looked at the glass from the exterior side of the building. In this way, you would experience distorted images and never recognize people's faces or bodies directly, making people feel comfortable and not exposed when they shop. When you were inside the shopping area and looked out, you would experience a beautiful distorted image like an impressionistic painting with amazing colored light beams coming in.

From one side of the building at the entrance area, it had a diagonal hole that went the whole way through the different floor levels in the building to the rooftop. It functioned as a connector in the building.

The street motif is powerful in front of the building with cars passing by at high speed, and sometimes pedestrians are walking by. Because of that, it was essential to have small public areas where people could sit and rest. One part was placed at the building entrance, and the other part was integrated with a sort of urban park.

I think people would feel fancy and get excited about the space in the building. We tried in the design to encourage this excitement. That is the main idea of the building design with the undulated glass façade for the Louis Vuitton competition.

The project was a part of a competition, but the client did not choose any winning entry at all. Later, the assignment was handed over to Frank Gehry's office, and the design by their office, which also uses undulated glass, is now built.

Recently, BCHO Partners finished a project at a different site near that fashion district, with a similar kind of undulated glass. It was impossible to find a company here in South Korea or China that could produce that kind of glass, so we found a good company in Spain near Barcelona that had the skills.

How were your expectations when you went into the Hyundai GBC competition project? Did you expect this huge project ever to be built?

Ji-hyun: Honestly, I expected it just to be a competition, and having participated in this competition in and of itself meant something to me.

The site and the volume of the whole complex were huge, and I guess Hyundai wanted a master architect to control every aspect of the overall organization and planning.

Previously, an international competition with famous international architects had already been held before us. The organizers, however, did not like the proposed schemes, so another domestic competition was arranged with five selected teams—and we actually won the competition.

The plan included two skyscrapers and two small towers with a public auditorium, a cultural center, and an extensive public park. In total, there were a lot of different kinds of programs involved. The tallest skyscraper was 105 stories high and was expected to be the highest in Asia to be built at that time.

Our scheme was unique and completely different from the other participants' scheme, in that two skyscrapers are positioned along the central boulevard in Gangnam, making the streetscape more coherent and integrated.

Although our proposal won the first prize and appreciation from the jury, we heard the news that Hyundai had engaged Skidmore, Owens & Merrill for the actual design, probably due to their richer experience in skyscraper design.

Can you tell more about how you integrated the Hyundai GBC competition project with the dense urban site conditions in the heart of Seoul?

Byoung: In the Hyundai GBC competition, the land was essential, especially how the design proposal was interwoven with the surrounding small existing buildings. Hyundai, a giant corporation, was the owner of this centrally located plot in Seoul's Gangnam district. Potentially, the project could metaphorically have been like a destructive cancer cell embedded in the city's heart, so that is why we carefully tried to weave the site of the competition with the surrounding city, because of a consideration of the cityscape's overall quality.

The site is a big piece of land of about 645,835 square feet (60,000 square meters) in a dense urban area in Gangnam. We were worried that the project could block many views and experiences in the city, so we lifted the project from the ground. In this way, all the existing urban fabric with small streets and shops continued on the site under the platform, and we created a kind of urban park above. The main lobby for the central tower started from this upper platform level. The lower level pretty much remained accessible to the public with open activities like shops, restaurants, and cafés, so people really could use this lower part like any other urban area. We made an opening in the middle of the plateau for the sunlight to penetrate, which created a nice pedestrian boulevard. In that way, there would be natural light underneath and, in the park, above.

The jury thought this was an excellent idea that would operate very well. The Hyundai company thought Skidmore, Owings & Merrill, an office much experienced in high-rise buildings, should be commissioned for the job. Of course, it is a pity we were not involved in the continuous process, but we learned much from it and showed that the office could design that type of large-scale projects.

How did you feel about the unexpected procedure behind the project?

Byoung: In this specific project, Seoul City was the part that pushed Hyundai to arrange an invited competition with five architects selected by Seoul City themselves. Hyundai probably wanted to engage a big established company like Skidmore, Owings & Merrill from the beginning because they had worked together before, so it would be easier for them to continue this cooperation. Seoul City could not force Hyundai to involve us even though the competition guidelines announced that we would be part of some of the project as winners of the competition—but it did not go that way.

As an architect, do you think you got caught in a political game between a huge corporate company like Hyundai and the Seoul City government?

Byoung: Big competitions always get complicated. In the end, Hyundai changed their mind and decided to go for a new scheme with three lower buildings of sixteen stories, rather than super-tall high-rises, because it is more economical and sustainable.

The memory of the unbuilt

Let us move to your experience and personal memory of unbuilt projects. How do you remember the unbuilt project you have been involved with? Is it the design concept, or is it the unredeemed process?

Ji-hyun: I have to say most of the projects by BCHO Partners have been built or are going to be built, so I do not have many experiences with unbuilt projects. But I believe some of the unbuilt projects that I was in charge of, were definitely a part of the learning process.

For instance, there were quite a few cases in which projects were canceled and unbuilt because the clients passionately focused on profitability. But even that is part of architecture, dealing not only with physical/materialistic quality but also with economic factors.

Ja-yoon: It depends on the characteristics or stage of the project. Early concept design projects or competition projects are memorable in the process of studying in finding unique design solutions (concepts) for a given site and design requirements. The original proposed site of the AYU25 Botanical Café was a flat land overlooking mountains and rivers. A sloped platform with a central courtyard was proposed to make the surrounding nature experience more dramatic. After the concept proposal, the site was changed to a large land with similar relationships between rivers and mountains, making it impossible to use the original design. However, through the previous study process, we came up with a more advanced concept and proposed a design suitable for the new land.

The CGV Warehouse Renovation project was a big learning lesson regarding the complex process of persuading large corporate clients and Incheon City to create projects open to the public.

 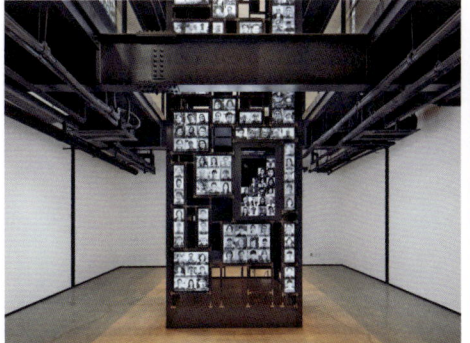 

Gwangju 518 Memorial (2015)

Kyung-jin: For two years in my early career at BCHO Partners, I worked on one project. It was the most extensive project I have been working on at BCHO Partners. In that project, there were five buildings on a site which is a famous historical place in Gwangju located in the southern part of South Korea. In the 1970s, people in that region were fighting against dictatorship for democracy. Many people died during that time, which made the site an important historical location. We worked on the renovation of five buildings in a complex with the old local government building, which was the place for the dramatic incident.

While working on this project, I worked with many interesting people, including a poet, a stage artist, a cultural heritage repair engineer, and so on. I would never have met these people because they are not naturally related to my everyday life. To generate ideas and proceed with the project, I came across a lot of exciting moments.

I found it especially interesting to see how different it is for people of various backgrounds to look at history and interpret it in their own ways: into the beautiful texts by a poet, into the metaphorical scene by a stage artist, into the redefined old space by an architect. The key to the project's success seemed to depend on how these ideas would intermingle with each other into one, but this was not an easy task. For example, when I worked on the project, there were not so many adaptive reuse projects in Korea as there are now. At the time, the cultural heritage repair expert was so conservative that they did not allow us to change anything. We, as architects, interpreted the historical site and wanted to make space reborn, not as a replica of a historical site but as a live space. If this project had been carried out today, our suggestion might have gained much more consensus rather than opposition. Compared to the time and effort devoted to this project, the outcome of this project does not stand out in that only three buildings out of five were realized. It was because of the opposition by cultural heritage experts and the bereaved families of the victims. Unfortunately, it was impossible to experience most of the ideas built, but I felt lucky to have worked with enthusiastic artists and enjoyed the creative working process. Above all, in this project, I learned the character of the memory of the site and buildings is up to the architect, artist, and the families of the victims.

Yerie: After a certain amount of time passed, what I remember as most important with unbuilt projects is the people's relationship during the process. The memorable thing about the Buddhist temple project in Texas was the relationship with people. As I previously said, the client was a religious organization, and the people connected to the organization were very gentle monks. So, it was a precious experience to work with respectful people.

However, since no architect wants to keep their project unbuilt, unbuilt projects cannot stay only in good memory. Architecture is a field of art based on the realization of an idea. It is hard to forget a project's original architectural idea because every architect builds their project in every step in their minds, whether built or unbuilt. That is why it is hard to forget projects.

From the initial design concept to more detailed ideas, every step is essential during the design process. So it's hard to say that a certain part of the design process of an unbuilt project is more memorable or difficult to forget.

For the Houston-based Buddhist Cultural Center and Dormitory, I have studied the local architectural style and tried to apply it to our design as well. The development process of the semi-open space of the main entrance is still vivid. It started from a 16-foot (5-meter) extended roof with several columns and developed into a semi-open space with repeated fine louvers.

For the Sampyo Headquarters project, we developed the design as well as technical or structural elements. Together with the structural engineers in the company's precast department, we studied several technical issues. One of them was how to obtain structural stability to lateral loads despite its innate instability as part of a collective of structural elements. Another issue was to avoid water leakage, especially for the basement construction, and finally, how to minimize the weight of precast façade panels while sustaining its design quality.

Even though certain architectural values can only be learned after the construction begins, the knowledge and experience we've earned from the design process of unbuilt projects are cherished as much as from built projects.

When we talk about unbuilt projects, do you think it is possible to detect some kind of patterns for the process to fail?

Yerie: It is difficult to say that there is a pattern for unbuilt projects. These unbuilt projects always result from sudden unexpectedness. But, if a project is on hold, the reasons could be different according to the scale of a project.

The larger a project is, the more challenging it becomes to start and accomplish and more challenging to stop again. It creates conflicts when many stakeholders are involved as if a project has some sort of physical inertia. For private clients with small projects, it is easier to start and easier to stop because it is only based on one client's will to continue or not. Sometimes, a client wants to perceive it further, invest more money in the project, or the economic situation changes, and the client's business becomes terrible, which makes it all stop. In that case, it is based on the situation and often one person's mind.

Ji-hyun: I have also been doing quite big-scale projects at BCHO Partners, and some of the projects were stopped due to the potential lack of profitability.

For instance, in the Sampyo Headquarters project, there have been many disagreements and conflicts between the City Council Committee and the client's side regarding the number of public housing units, which causes a significant profit difference. So, the program of the whole complex was adjusted many times between offices, commercial facilities, and the housing units. Until those factors are final decided, the project cannot proceed any further.

Ja-yoon: I worked on the Dana Point Hotel project in Los Angeles. A developer connected us to the client to develop a hotel, so we went to study the fantastic plot located on a cliff at the ocean site. The idea of our design with the hotel project started from the shape of the ground, creating plateaus so that every room would have an ocean view, and it also had an internal green plaza. Our scheme's developer suggested that the landowner provide the financial investment. The landowner was interested in the design we presented to him, and we agreed to formalize a contract soon, but he then broke the connection. It is said he hired a local architect who developed a similar scheme at a very low budget. It is a disappointing story for this project.

Byoung: It always depends on the character of the project. In the end, the financial aspect is often a dominant factor for stopping projects. At other times there might be a strong political struggle within a company. It also happens that the owner of a big corporation changes their mind for some reason. For example, in the Buddhist Cultural Center and Dormitory project in Houston they didn't have money at the time because they prioritized other buildings first. I had a feeling that the temple organization was internally divided with different interests. People in the local branch in Texas wanted this project built. The main branch with more power thought it was a very nice proposal, but it was perhaps too new and inventive for them, even though we met the budget. Decision makers in the main branch were in charge of the budget, and members didn't vote for the scheme but for another project. In South Korea, most projects do not have such a complicated organizational structure. They are controlled by one person: an owner or a CEO.

Overall, it varies what makes projects unbuilt, but the financial aspects are, of course, one of the main reasons.

Importance of unbuilt projects

Finally, I am curious about how the unbuilt projects influence the work and the artistic creativity of the office?

Byoung: I consider unbuilt projects, exhibitions, and experiments in a scale 1:1 to be an essential factor in the activities and creative processes that exists in an architectural office. At BCHO Partners, we emphasize the symbiosis of these activities with the built architecture.

Besides being involved in designing and constructing architecture for clients, the office is also engaged in different activities that stress the importance of cultural development.

A general positive thing with unbuilt projects where clients are involved is the maintenance and expansion of contacts and networks for future engagements. Unbuilt projects also expose the clarity of the original concept more powerfully before pragmatic elements start a process of blurring the idea. However, it might be that in architectural competitions, you encounter more substantial elements of creative experiments, especially what is concerning techniques of representation.

Earth House Jedong Ranch mediation space Jipyoung Guesthouse

Making competitions in a very short and intensive period might feel challenging, but afterward, it transfers energy and ideas to future projects. Competitions display creativity and make the office be part of the cultural development in an ever-changing world.

The office has built several concept houses through the years that explore different and fundamental aspects of architecture. It is an excellent way to experiment with space, construction, and materiality in a scale 1:1. Best known is Earth House, a house built on the idea to commemorate the late Korean poet Dong-ju Yun. The house uses the open space "*mahdahng*" originally found in the middle of the traditional Korean courtyard house but placed underground, giving room for meditation and poem readings. The ideas of Earth House have been pursued and implemented in later buildings like Geoji-do Guesthouse from 2018.

Another way to explore potentials in architecture is to make and participate in exhibitions. It has been very fortunate for the office to be involved in the activities around Onground Gallery. The engagement has made it possible to arrange exhibitions and invite national and foreign architects to contribute. These activities contribute to an exchange of ideas that is fruitful for the creativity of the office. BCHO Partners has published several books and an extensive monograph about the office's work in connection to the exhibitions. I think these book projects function as reflective flashbacks that put things in perspective and have the potential to lead a direction toward the future.

In my opinion, all of these various activities are important to establish vitality and positive development within a creative office.

I also hope with this book that the architectural ideas and creative processes of BCHO Partners will be experienced with clarity in the unbuilt projects displayed.

JOONGANG-CHUNG MUSEUM

Making visible the scars of a powerful force that once fractured Korea's national identity

Jongno District, Seoul, Korea | 2018

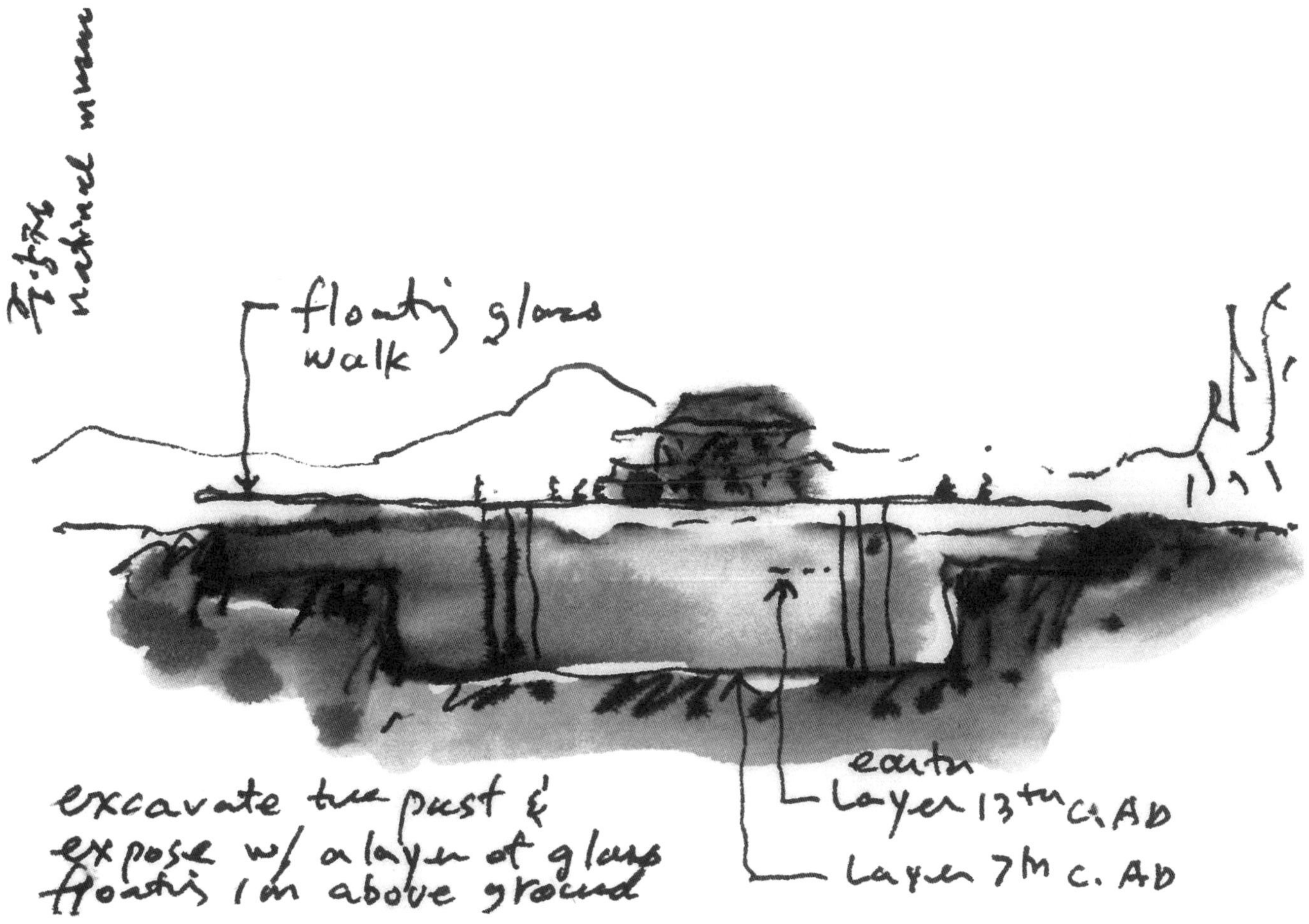

Tigris natural museum

floating glass walk

excavate the past &
expose w/ a layer of glass
floating 1m above ground

earth
Layer 13th c. AD
Layer 7th c. AD

Joongangchung Museum

The Japanese Government-General Building (Joongangchung; built in 1929) was located inside Gyeongbokgung Palace, behind the Gwanghwamun gate. Following Korea's liberation from Japanese imperial rule in 1945 at the end of World War II, it was used as the Korean Government-General Building and it housed the National Museum of Korea from 1986, but today there is no trace of the Japanese Government-General Building's existence. Its demolition was ordered during the Kim Young-sam administration, and completely demolished in 1996:

> "We are here to confirm the demolition of the Japanese Government-General Building, the headquarters of enforcing colonial policies that destroyed the language, history, and lives of our people. Today, we solemnly proclaim the restoration work of the Main Palace and the construction of a new Cultural Street, seeking unification and a brighter future by burying this dismal past and straightening out our national spirit."
>
> *Proprium* (August 15, 1995)

Gwanghwamun was originally built during the Joseon Dynasty. Once the Japanese Governor-General of Korea was removed, Gwanghwamun was rebuilt, but the gate was newly constructed with contemporary materials, marking the beginning of a new history.

Few would disagree with the decision to demolish the Japanese Government-General Building and to restore Gwanghwamun to its former appearance; the site was seen to be a symbol of the social and cultural traumas of Japanese imperialism. We feel, however, that the history of this scar demands that we should be recording it in detail in some way as opposed to erasing it entirely. The sufferings under the rule of the Japanese Empire must be marked and remembered, so that we can truly embark upon a new line in history. Time only runs forward and it can never be modified, so no building can be restored once demolished. Therefore, we believe that the traces of history, such as those impressions left by the Japanese Government-General Building and its fence, should remain on permanent record.

Joongangchung Museum

The existing courtyard, located in the center of the Joongangchung, sits 20 feet (6 meters) belowground. The calmly descended space symbolizes the layers of historical events and meanings stacked on this land. The sharp spatial presence that one experiences while walking on the transparent glass plate and the shape of heavily fallen structures makes one realize that this place was once a scene of pain.

Joongangchung Museum

Upon arrival at the underground museum and as one looks up toward the sky, one is met with an intersection of brilliant light and shadow between the Gyeongbokgung Palace and Bukak Mountain. The series of spatial experiences memorialize the spirit of those who fiercely fought for our independence.

The preservation of the Japanese Government-General Building was a complex task, a powerful image of a force that once fractured Korea's national identity. Our view was that using the building as a museum (such as by simply placing exhibition contents inside its four walls) would be inadequate as a long-term educational prospect. Rather than a simple restoration or preservation project, we decided it was more important to disclose each and every piece of history in detail, and to allow visitors to experience and recognize this history throughout the site. In order to pass a sense of a national story on to the next generation, and to allow the site to act as an active field in which to experience history, we deemed it necessary to leave those traces visible rather than to completely demolish the building and all signs of its existence.

Joongangchung Museum

Sectional model (plywood, acrylic)

Sectional model (plywood, acrylic)

Joongangchung Museum

Our Joongangchung project proposed the preservation of the underground space of the Japanese Government-General Building by cutting off the building at 3.9 feet (1.2 meters) aboveground, covering the remaining horizontal surface with tempered glass, and allowing visitors to walk over it. Cutting off the building at this height and revealing its cross section would help people to see and reckon with the essence and impacts of the building more directly than via a simple shape seen from the outside. This design involved excavating the existing courtyard—located in the center of the old Japanese Government-General Building foundations—to 20 feet (6 meters) belowground and creating two empty spaces about 9.85 feet deep (3 meters deep), allowing people to experience the full historical strata of this site. Visitors would be able to see the layers of the Joseon Dynasty in the area of Gwanghwamun, and beneath that the ground of the previous Goryeo Dynasty.

Revealing the traces of history does not have to be vast in scale or ostentatious in manner. It should be sufficiently sensitive to its context, so that when our descendants or tourists visit this place they are able to recognize a critical moment in our culture, the marks of an oppressive period, and the struggle to reconcile the then and the now. It is important to bring not only a sense of history to view in a completely restored form, but also make visible a cross section of its traces. Looking back across history, we must strive to see the things that are often cast out of view or invisible. This project also aimed to regenerate the site as part of a revitalized city, encouraging visitors to experience the history of the site and the intriguing building erected here.

Joongangchung Museum

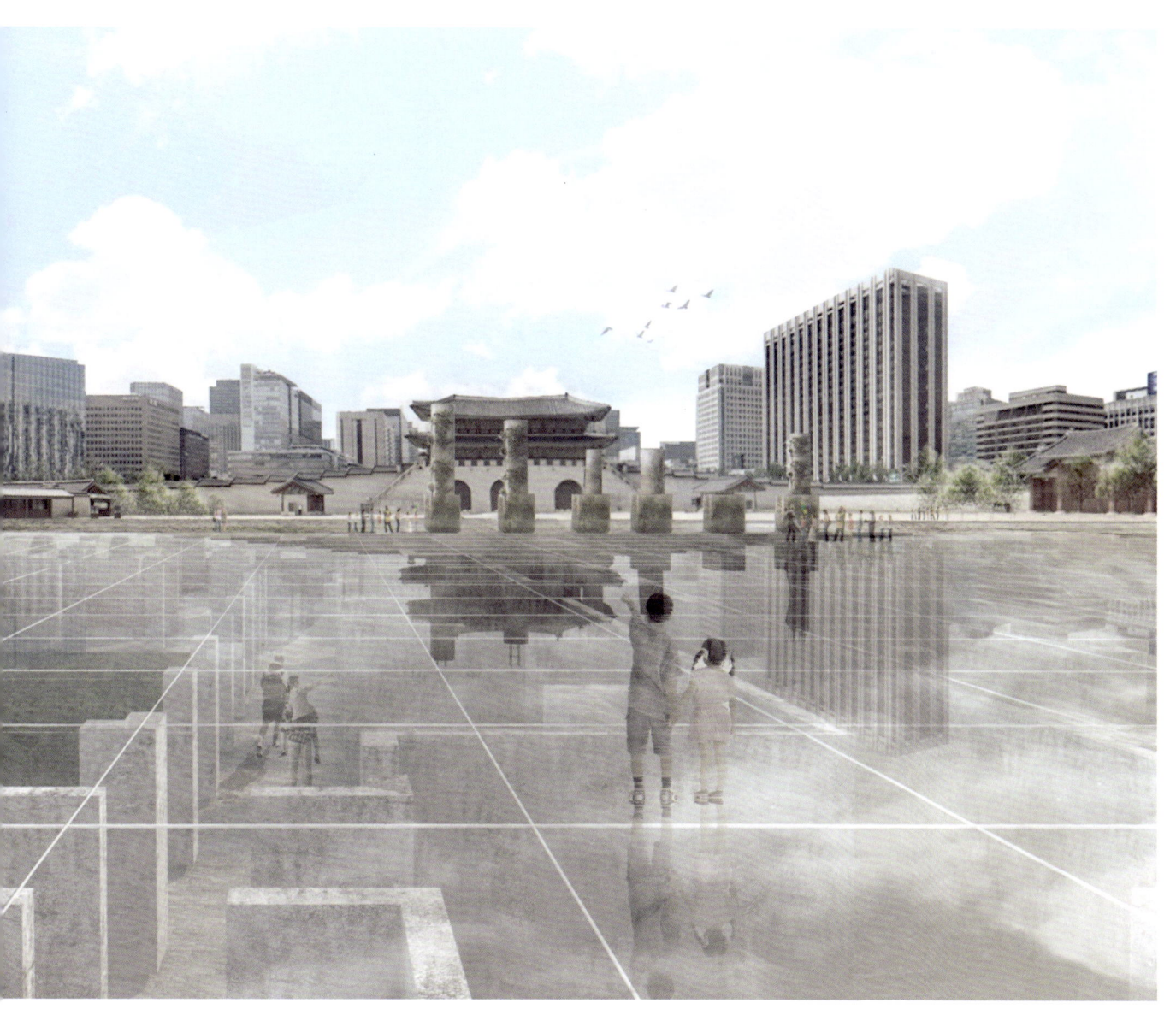

CGV WAREHOUSE RENOVATION

An urban passage that breathes life into an abandoned city landmark, creating new organic interactions, and connecting the urban fabric with time

Incheon, Gyeonggi Province, Korea | 2018

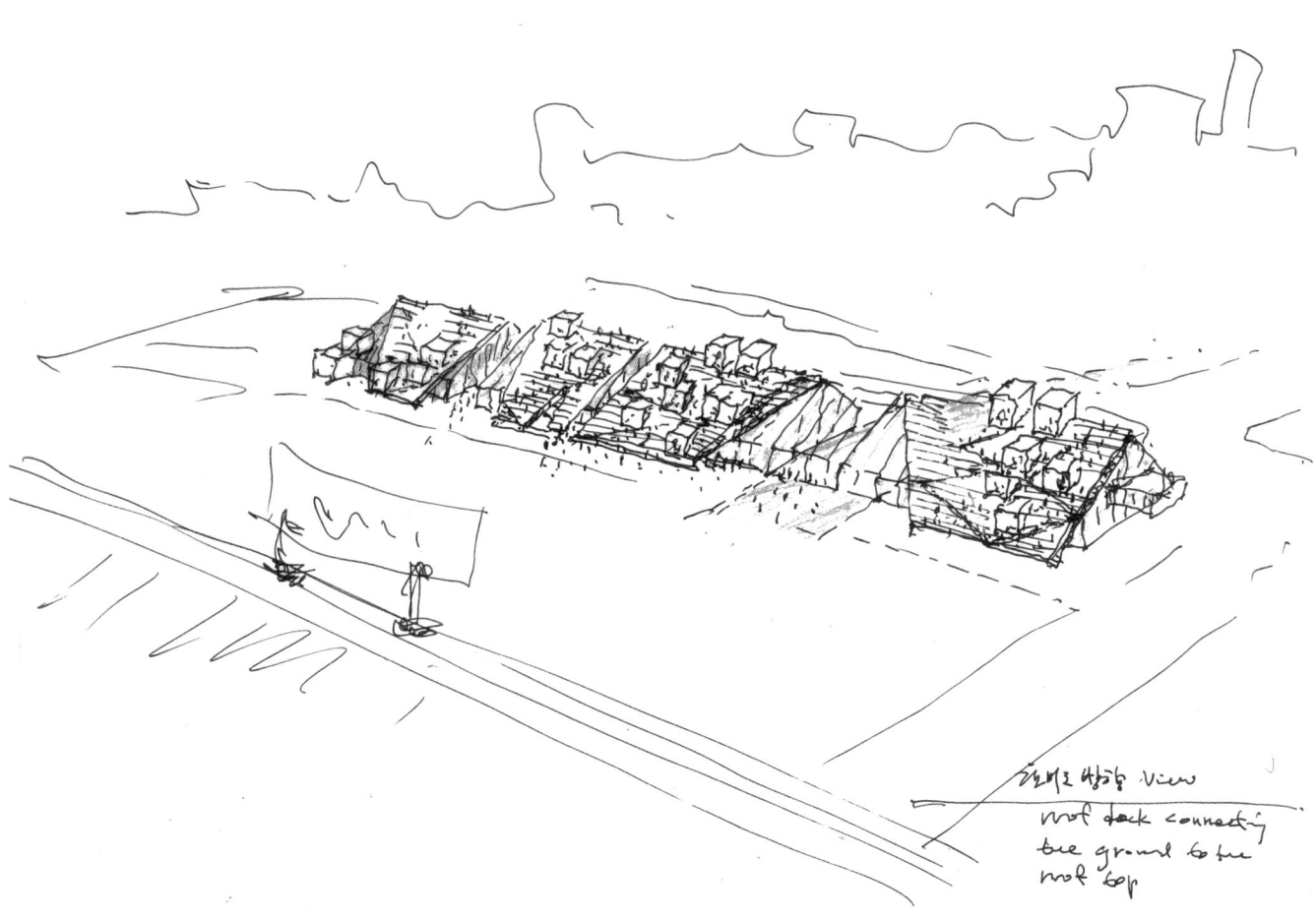

한강으로 바라본 view
roof deck connecting
the ground to the
roof top

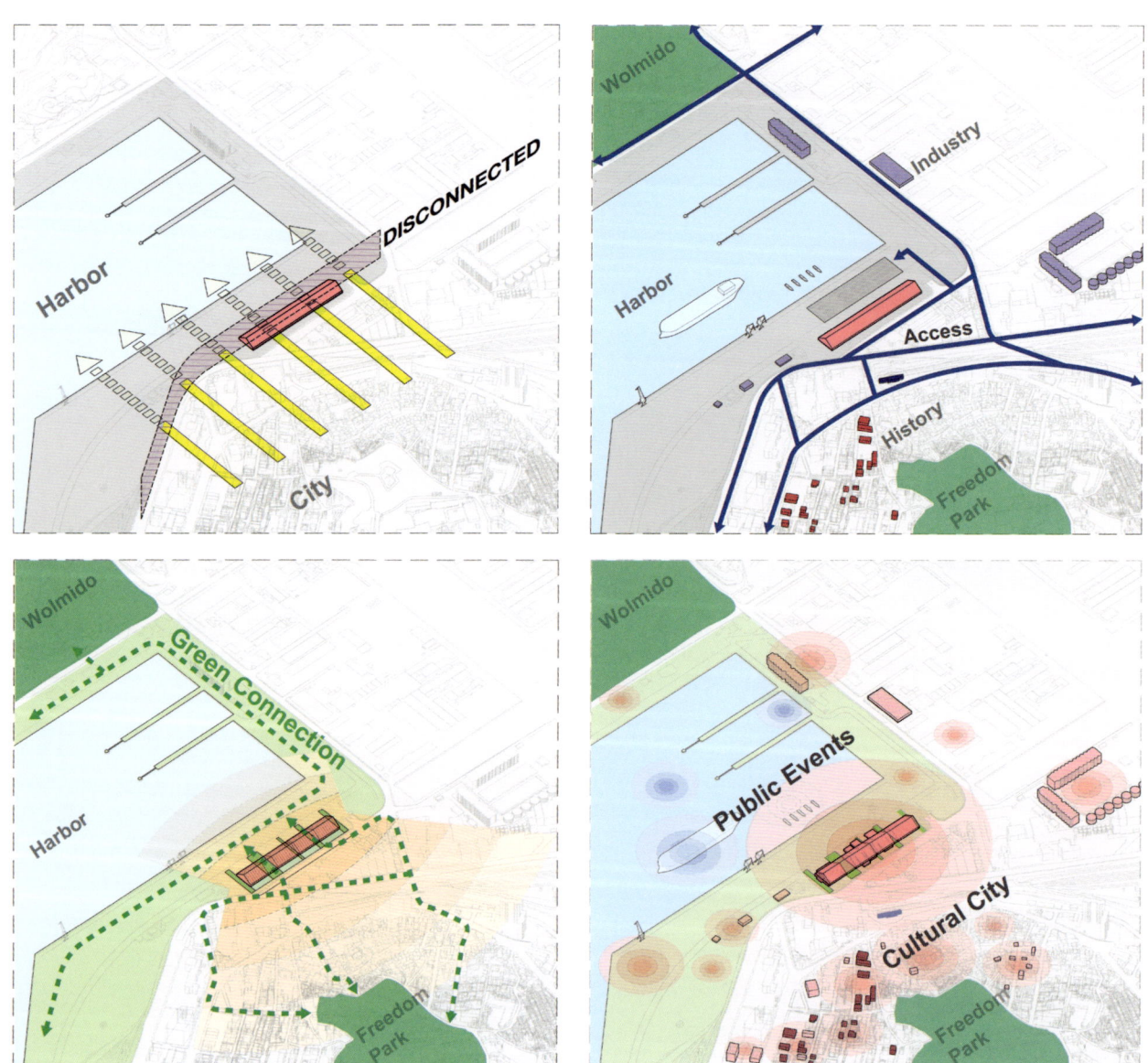

CGV Warehouse Renovation

The current architectural scene boasts a plethora of readaptive architecture that is often and easily misidentified with recycled architecture. We regard "resuscitation" as a more apt term to describe our work, which implies a new birth of an architectural identity. This steers away from the prevalent—and somewhat complacent—notion of simply reusing an existing structure. Rather, it demands from us, as architects, a dynamic reality in which the old and the new are held in organic interactions, collisions, and coexistence.

The site of our project, Incheon Pier 8, has long served as the country's center for maritime trade. It holds much historic significance, symbolizing South Korea's past century of modernization. Over time, however, its abandoned granary structure has become an obstacle, separating the city from its waterfront. The port's granary currently stands as a silent witness to the division left between the urban fabric and the waterfront by Incheon's former city planning phases. Through a series of architectural interventions, we sought to restore the fractured relationship between the urban fabric and the port by envisioning a new opportunity for the city's isolated waterfront, and thereby breathing new life into the port as a contemporary civic platform.

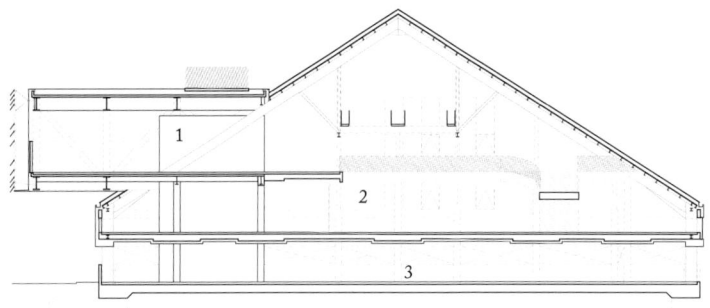

Cross section A–A

1. Entertainment center
2. Public
3. Parking

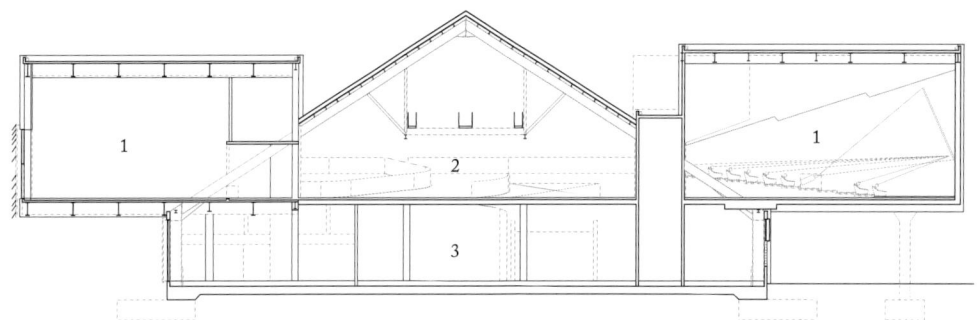

Cross section B–B

1. Cinema
2. Multipurpose hall
3. Aquarium

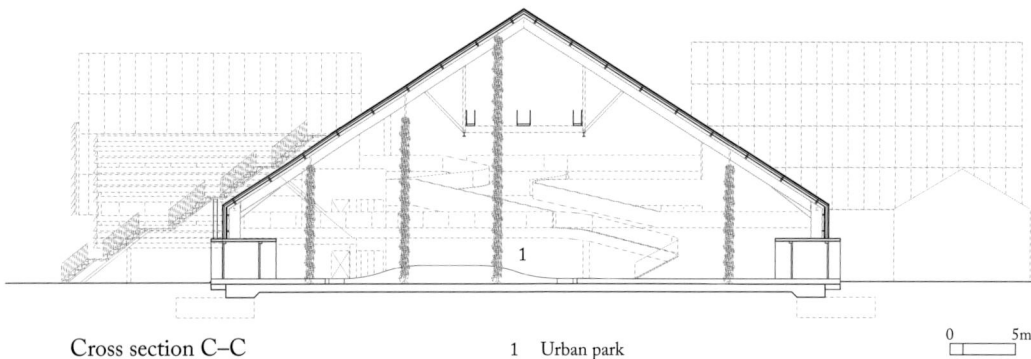

Cross section C–C

1. Urban park

CGV Warehouse Renovation

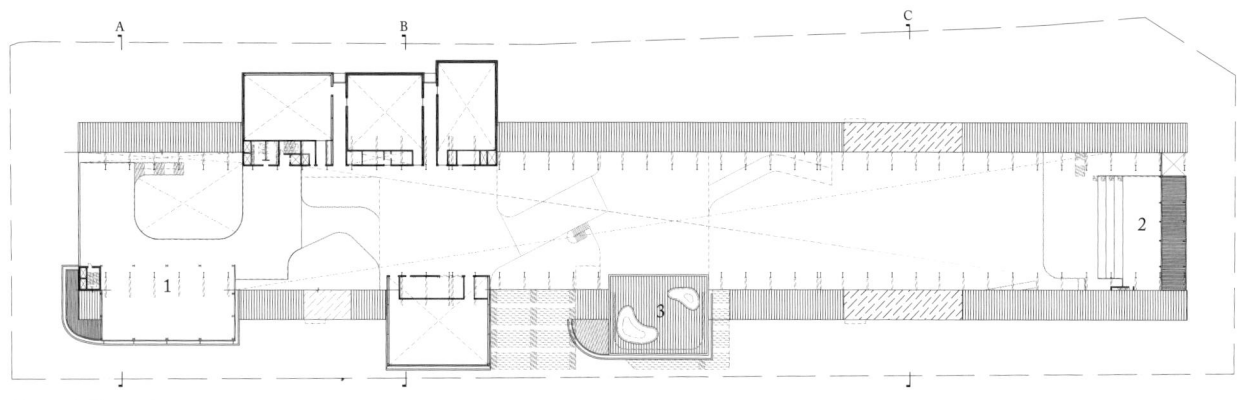

Second-floor plan

1 Entertainment center
2 Cafe / lounge
3 Rooftop garden

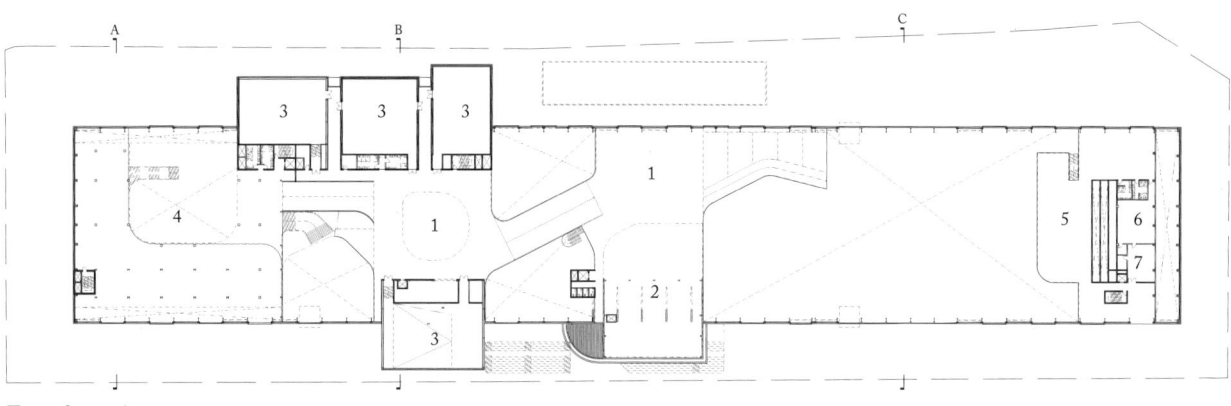

First-floor plan

1 Multipurpose hall
2 Dining
3 Cinema
4 Public
5 Café
6 Office
7 Education room

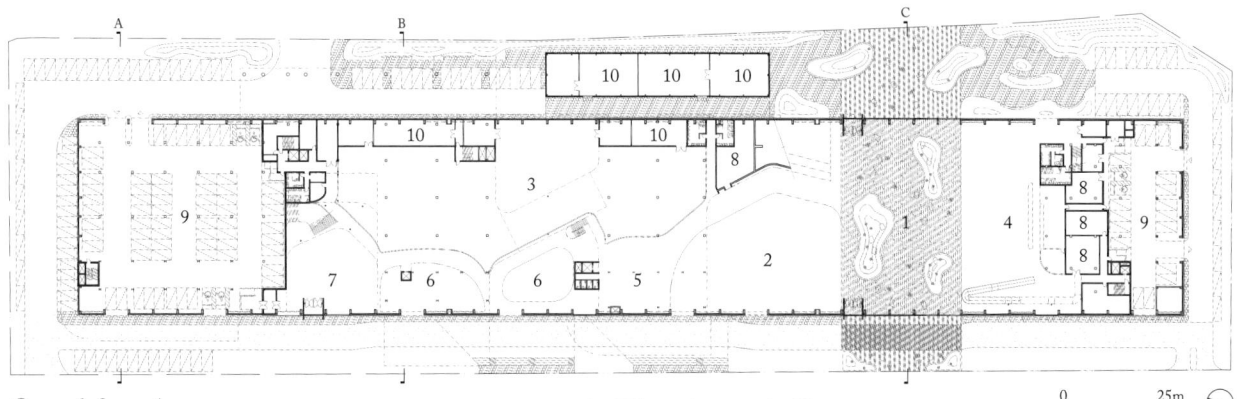

Ground-floor plan

1 Urban park
2 Dining
3 Aquarium
4 Café / bakery
5 Resting place
6 Shop
7 Public square
8 Office
9 Parking
10 MEP

CGV Warehouse Renovation

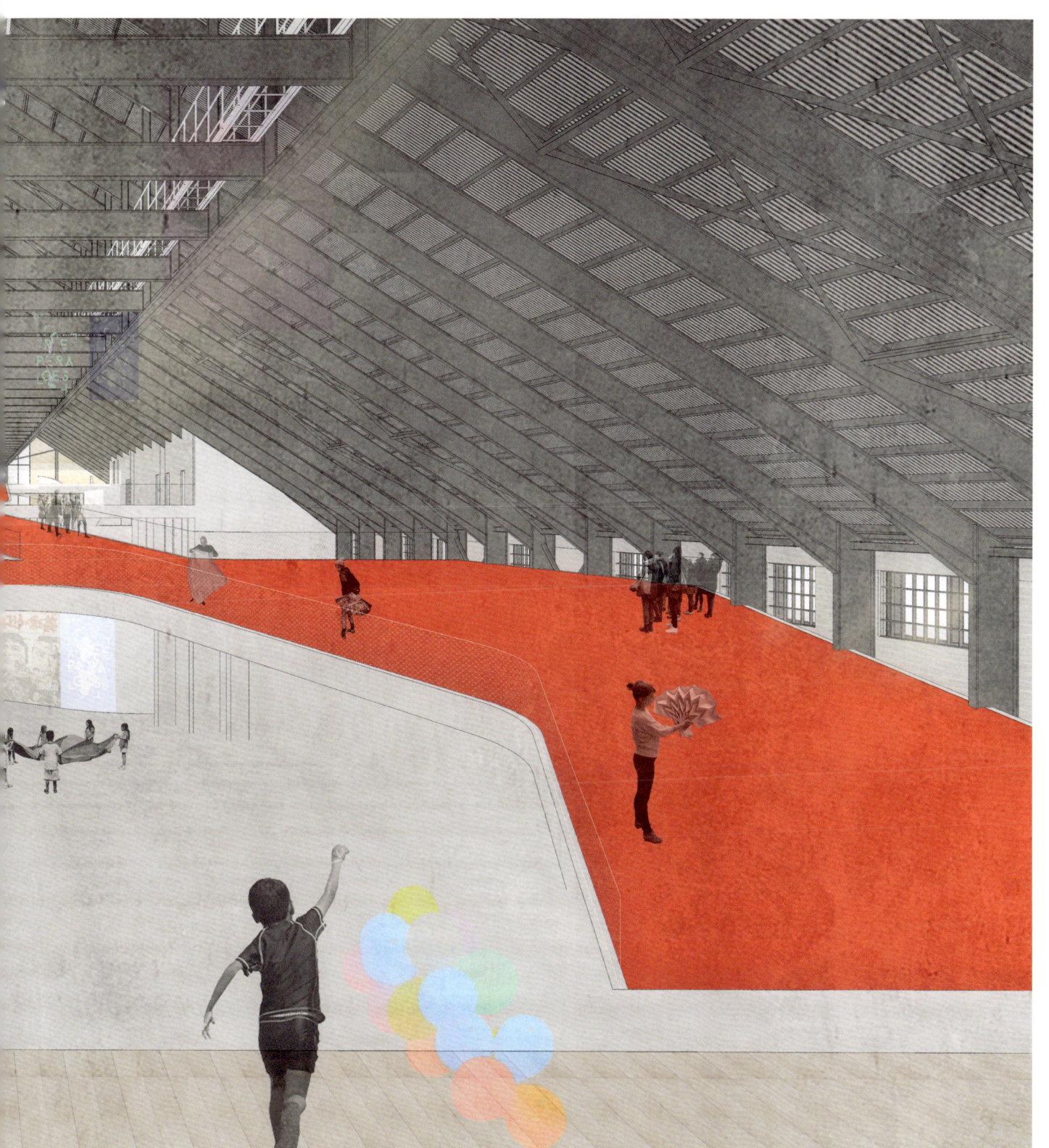

By cutting away the central mass of the granary, the once fractured flow of nature is now invited within in the form of a linear urban park. While preserving the building's main structure, the exterior finish is replaced with expanded metal screens and glass skylights, allowing for ample natural daylight to create an atmosphere like that of shadows beneath a giant tree. At the same time, gabion green poles and landscaping stones provide new contexts for various programmatic activities to take place, such as weddings, concerts, or other events. The juxtaposition of materiality, between the existing and the newly added, is gestural to an architectural identity that simultaneously acknowledges the past and responds to the future.

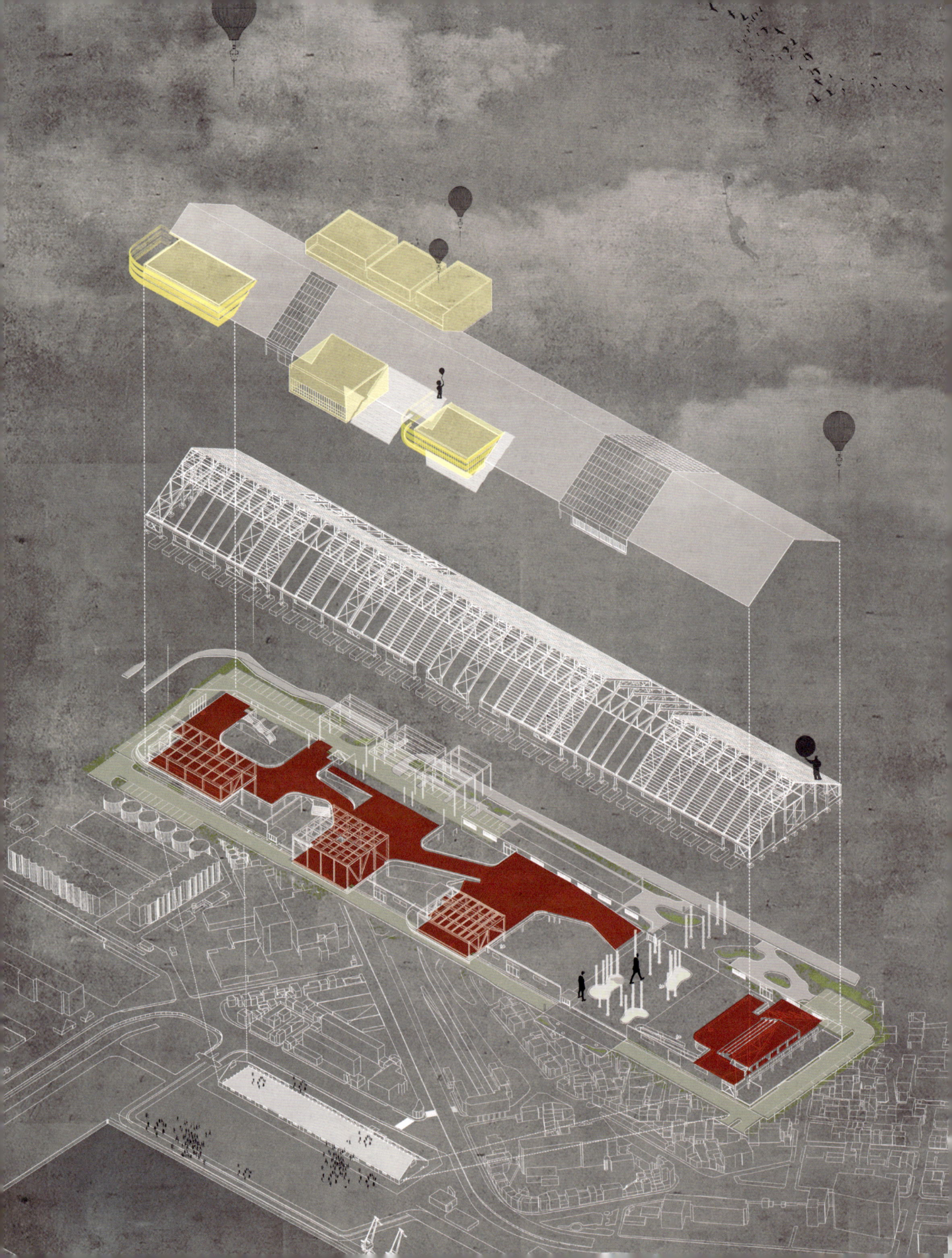

The scale of the columnless, single-building warehouse has no precedents in South Korea. The spatial qualities of this rather magical and cavernous space—being an overwhelming 886 feet long, 148 feet wide, and 64 feet high (270 meters long, 45 meters wide, and 19.5 meters high)—is experienced from a variety of levels and angles as visitors walk along the organic slopes of the interior platforms. Along this linear surface, different programmatic activities occur, loosely arranged and naturally divided by the platform's changing levels rather than by strict walls. By the time one arrives to the ramp end and turns around, the platform reveals its full length, unifying the entire warehouse into a single mass.

With the port being one of the city's most significant landmarks, we wanted to use the readaption of the granary to provide immersive views toward the port, facilitated by a set of framed, simple box-like spaces that would penetrate the existing structure. As the boxes dramatically push out of the pitched roofs along various levels, the surrounding port is captured in unique viewpoints. Perforated aluminum metal screens that wrap the programmatic boxes filter the sharpness of sunlight, while at night, interior lighting illuminates the boxes so that they become dynamic façades.

The flow that connects the city to the architecture and the architecture to the waterfront continues along the exterior roof of the granary. Huge carpet-like staircases cover the roof surface at a rather steep slope of about 1:1.6. Visitors are able to enjoy the unique experience of circulating up and across the surface of the building, and at times, enjoying the steps as public benches. With public access to the port long been prohibited, these staircases celebrate the rebirth of the granary as a truly public cultural complex.

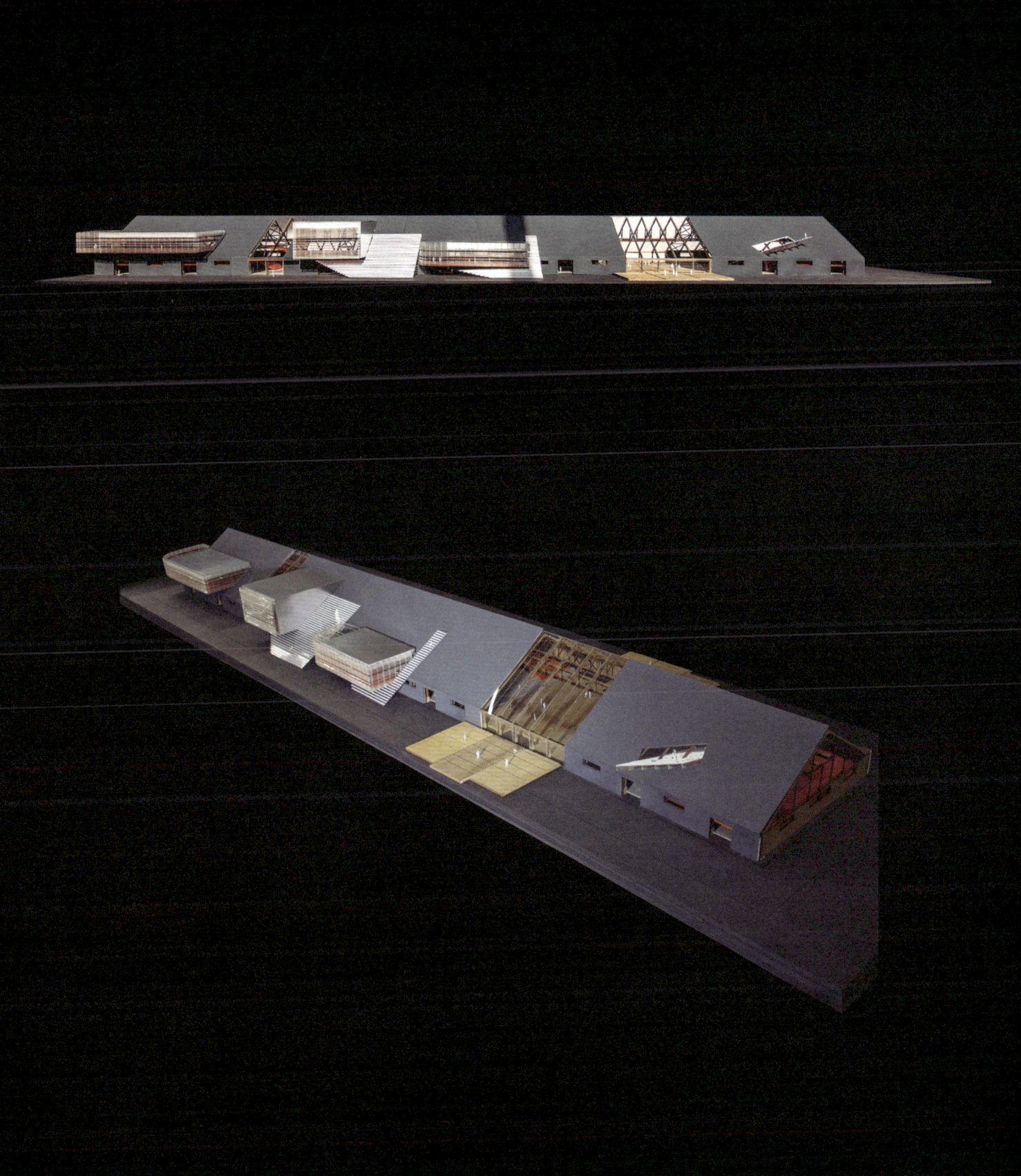

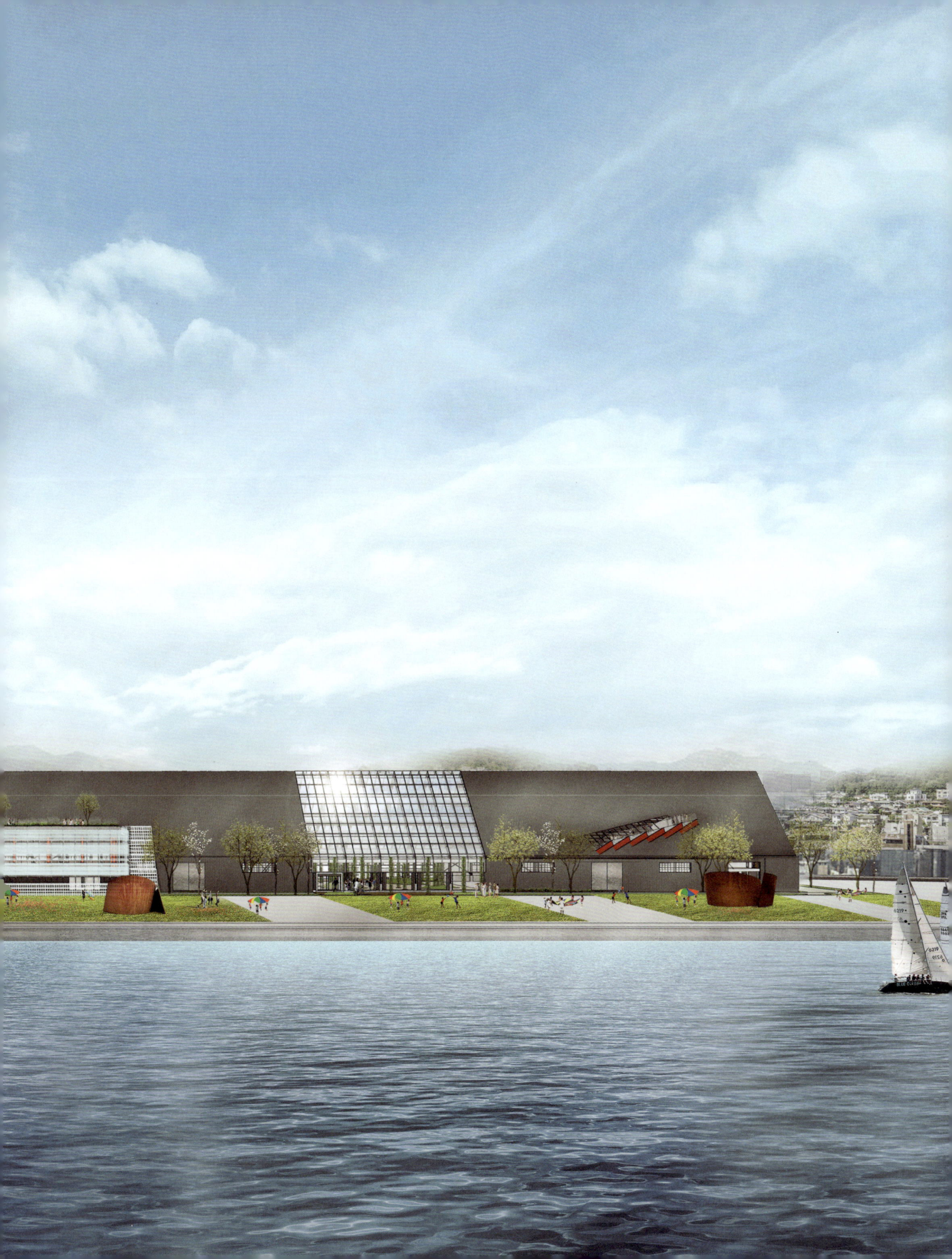

HYUNDAI MOTORS GBC

An organic, sustainable, and adaptive spatial configuration for an iconic landmark headquarters site

Seoul, Korea | 2016

Hyundai Motors GBC

This project comprised a monumental corporate landmark representing the visionary headquarters for Hyundai, proposed to embody Hyundai's iconic status and ambitious future vision. We designed a 105-story tower that would house more than 13,800 people by intertwining the existing programs surrounding the site. Following the scale and the unique patterns of the site's neighborhood, we created a responsive scale and program-driven concept to provide "spatial camouflage" for the project—particularly for the ground-floor areas—with various interconnections between the different programs. Our intent was to design a flexible spatial composition with an adaptive typology for the ground-floor areas to minimize the potential for the unwanted effect of uneven customer distribution often seen in other iconic high-rises in the area. Moreover, the small-scale spaces around the site were intended to hold a pleasing industrial artistic aesthetic, which would be attractive to shoppers and passersby.

The building's overall planning scheme was based on the bold gesture of generating a dynamic continuum in the cultural and commercial axis, with the flexible entry points and organic circulation throughout the site. The existing Seoul urban planning scheme prompted us to propose the internal pedestrian road to connect the sites east to west, which would establish a grand connection from Seoul's Coex Center to the Han River. The multiple vertical connections and circulation within the site would further connect the site to its neighborhood, allowing a better flow of people with a minimal discontinuity. Using the development's status as an urban connector, we wanted people to build an experience within their journey both in and out of the site, as well as for those who are passing by.

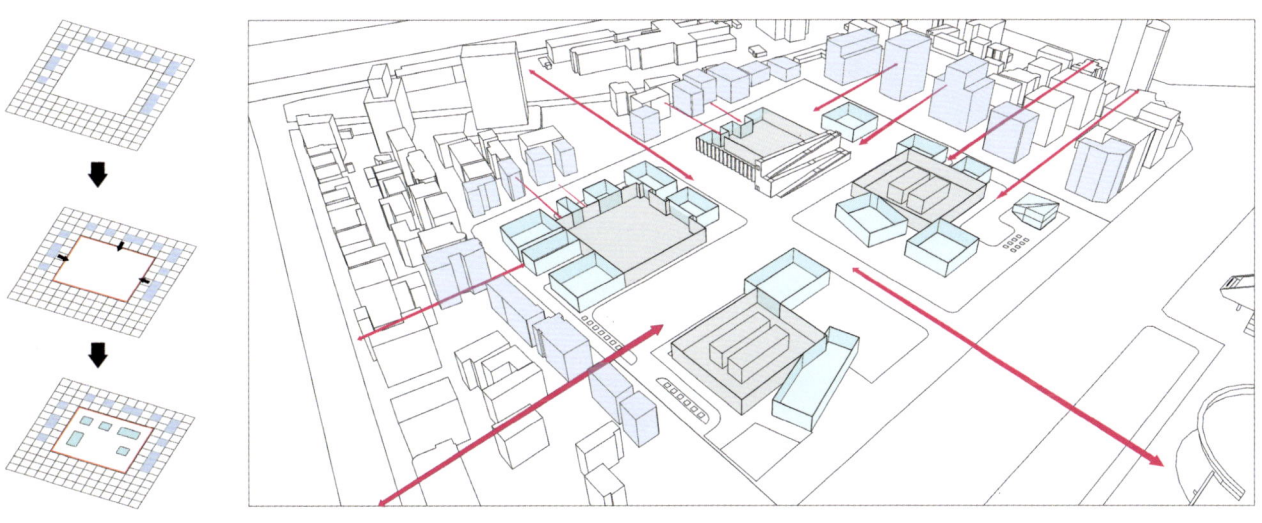

Hyundai Motors GBC

Hyundai Motors GBC

Hyundai Motors GBC

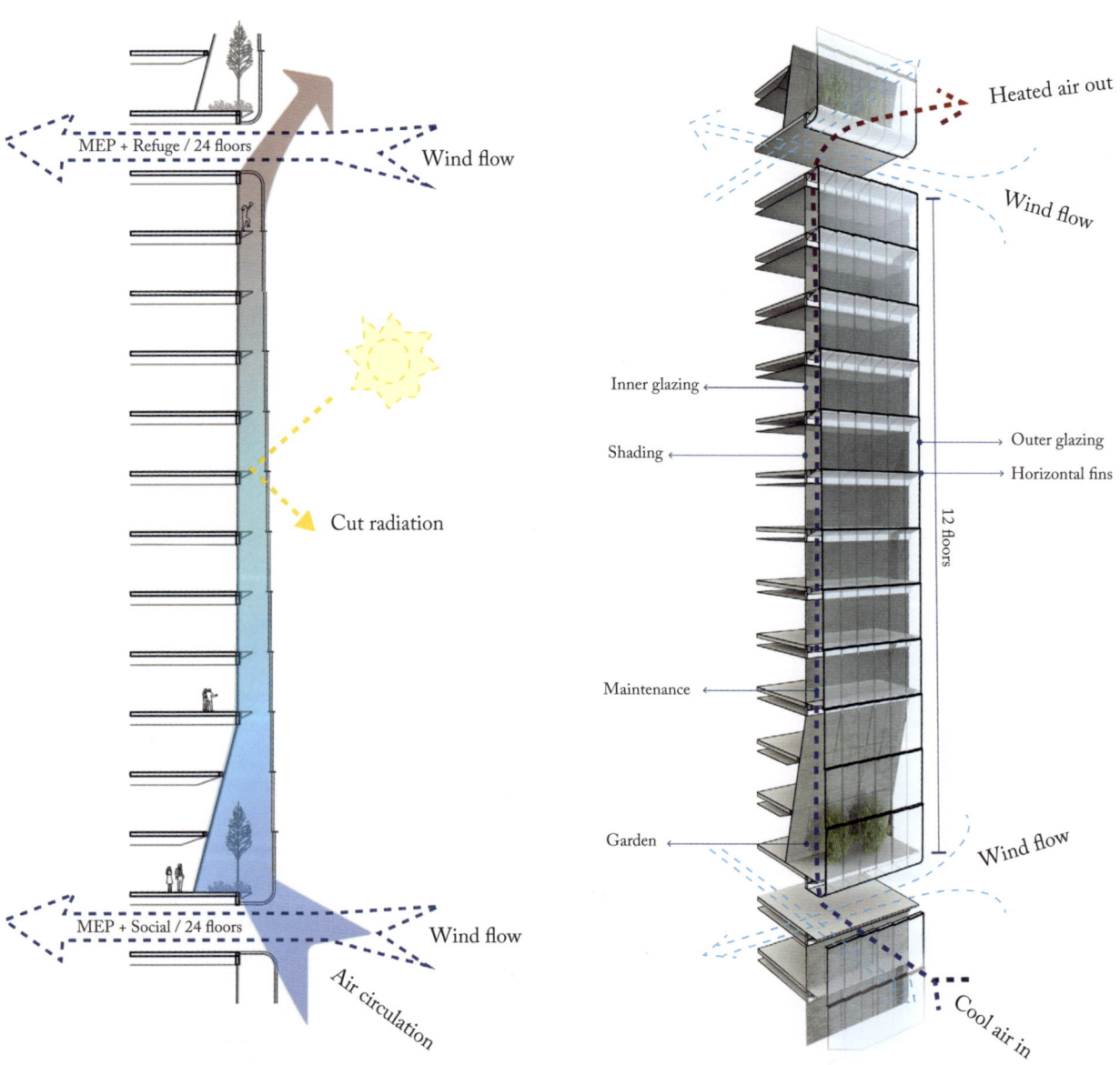

Hyundai Motors GBC

Each edge of the tower is smoothly sculpted by moving the tower's main supporting axis. The subtle round corners of the tower are to create a sustainable geometry, as well as for the internal spatial configuration. The vase-like geometry was a direct response to the building's solar impact and wind pressure at different heights. We focused on allowing maximum daylight penetration through the glass where necessary. Our minimal yet technologically packed and environmentally adaptive design proposed a mullion with its angle cleverly responding to the direction of the sun to maximize the building's efficiency. As part of a passive cooling strategy, the lower-level canopy above the main plaza offers natural ventilation with the double-skin façade systems on the upper parts of the tower. We installed vents every seven floors on the double-skin façade areas to create an efficient insulation layer that will release heat in summer and enclose heat in winter. Creating a garden space every seven floors also establishes a flexible spatial zone for busy workers to relax and enjoy the amazing views over the city.

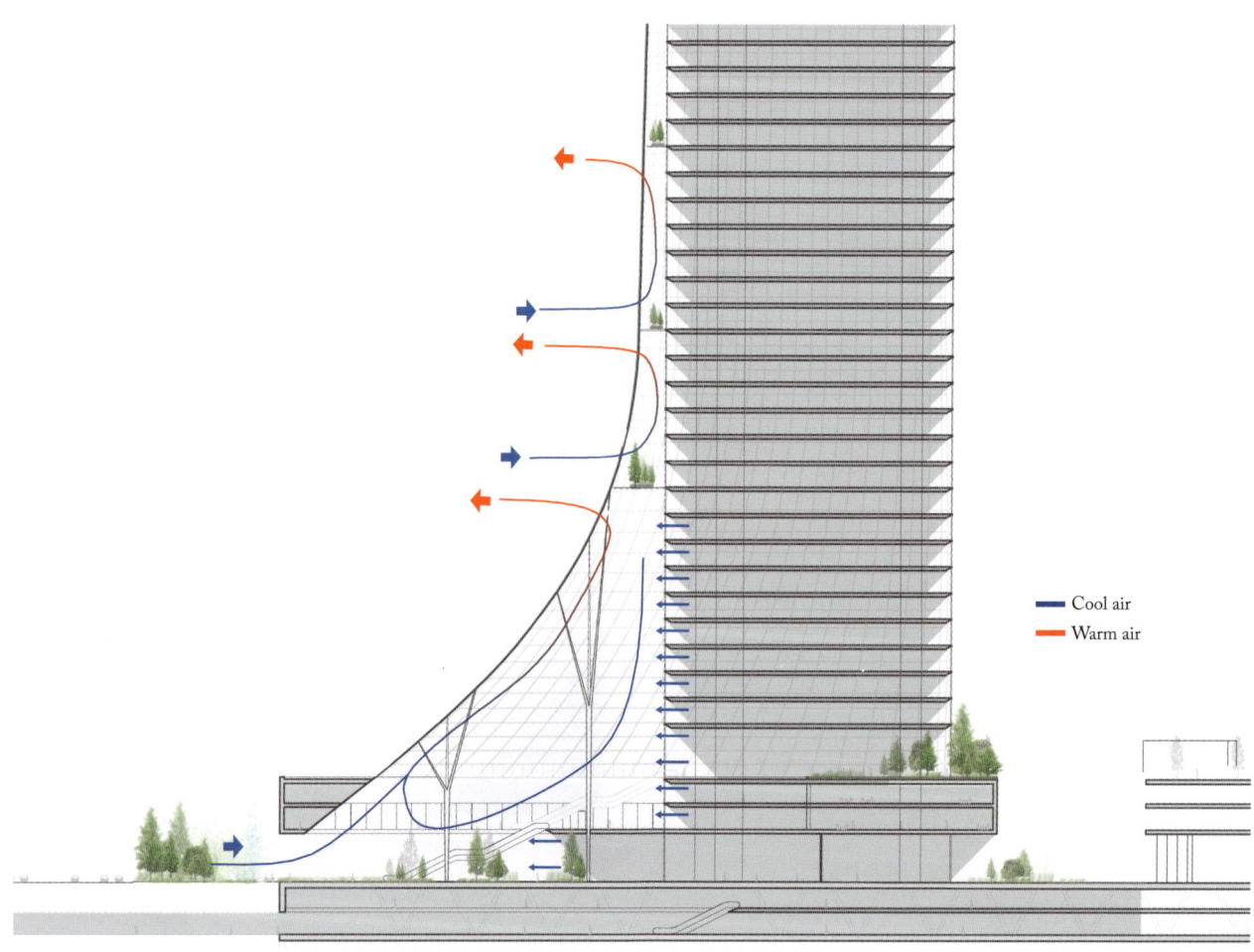

Hyundai Motors GBC

Hyundai Motors GBC

BUDDHIST CULTURAL CENTER AND DORMITORY

An invitation to enter an immersive experience that folds in architecture's communion and oneness with nature

Houston, Texas, United States | 2017

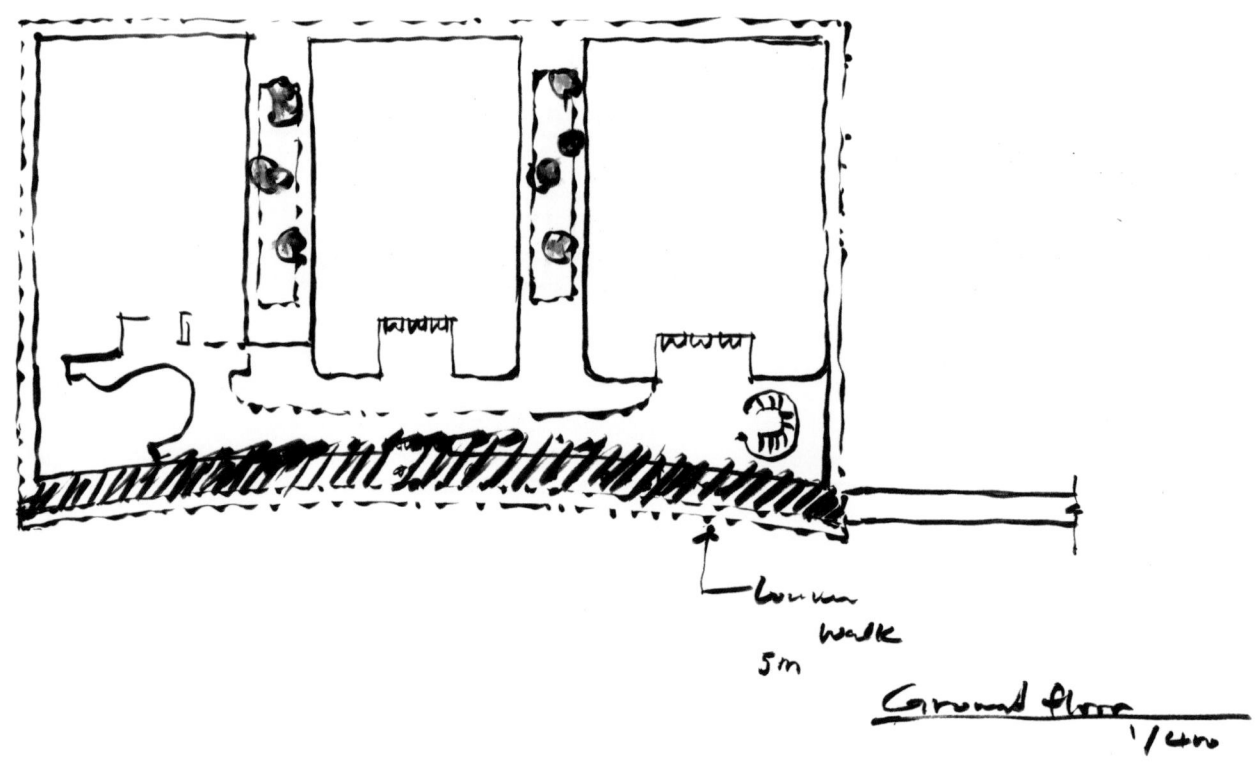

Buddhist Cultural Center and Dormitory

The new cultural center in Houston, Texas, United States, commissioned by the Fo Guang Shan International Buddhist Order, serves as one of the many worldwide branches established to promote awareness of and education about the Order's core values. The center comprises several programs, ranging from Buddhist services to symposia, lectures, and public events.

Our master plan proposal effectively responded to the scale and complexity of such operational demands, integrating the existing columbarium and dining hall with a newly proposed cultural center, guesthouse/dormitory, central plaza, and meditation forest.

Buddhist Cultural Center and Dormitory

The scheme references the environmental values of the Order, focusing on architecture's communion and oneness with nature. Architecturally, the buildings were designed to be climate responsive; filtering the harsh Texan daylight through aluminum screens. The detailed control of apertures also ensures optimal conditions for natural ventilation. From a planning point of view, the buildings are arranged in alignment with the innate axial conditions of the site, emphasizing order and harmony with their surrounding conditions. The vast expanse of the landscape and greenery planned between individual buildings invite visitors to enter an immersive experience for meditation and the appreciation of nature both within and outside the building.

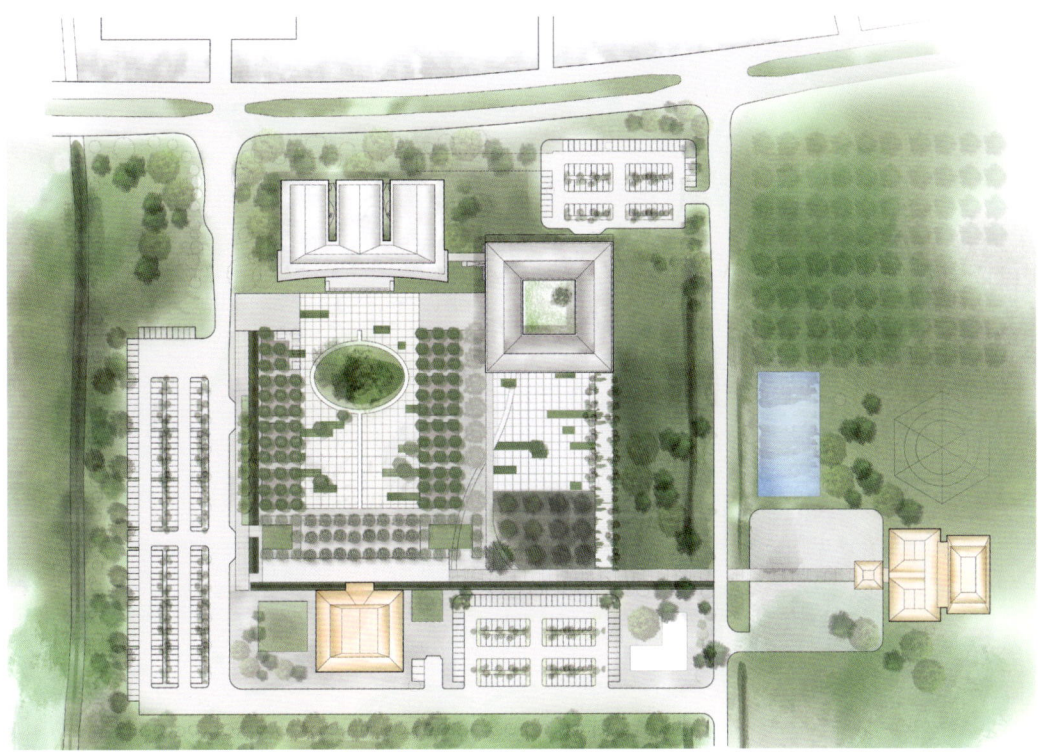

Master plan scheme 1

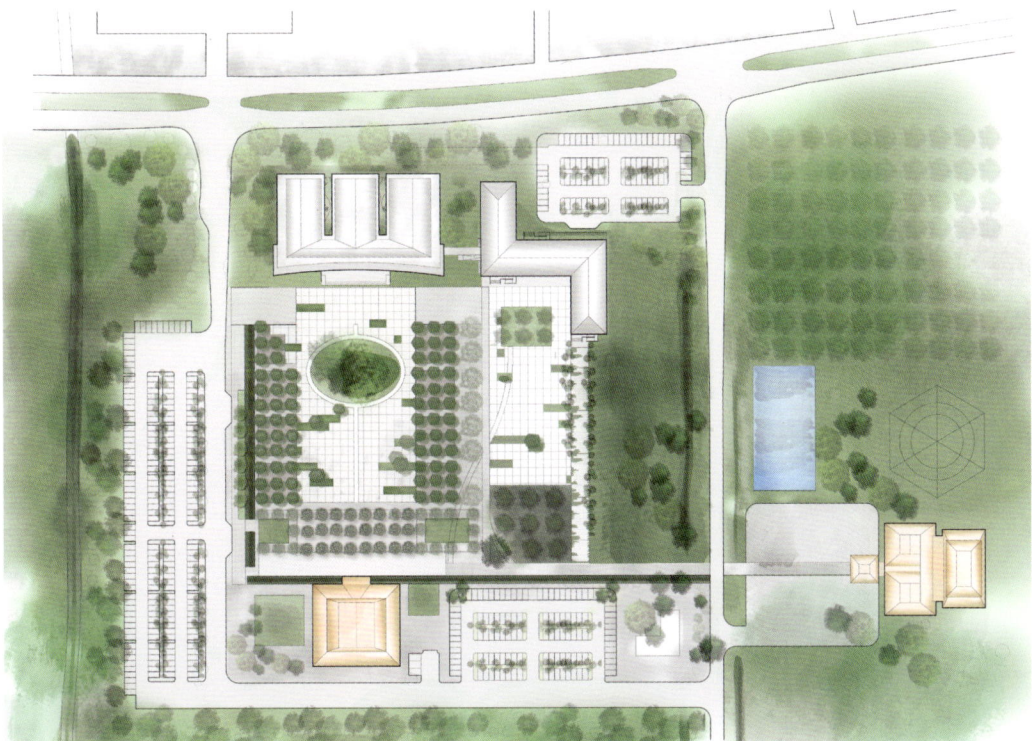

Master plan scheme 2

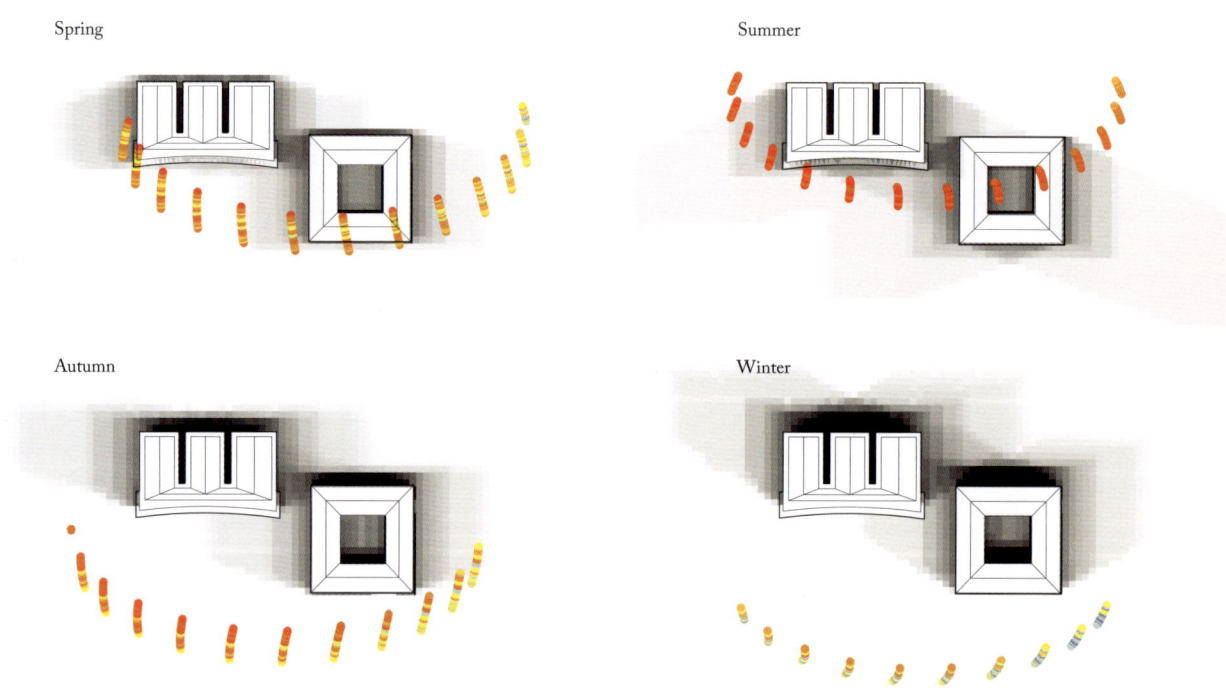

Seasonal solar modeling

Buddhist Cultural Center and Dormitory

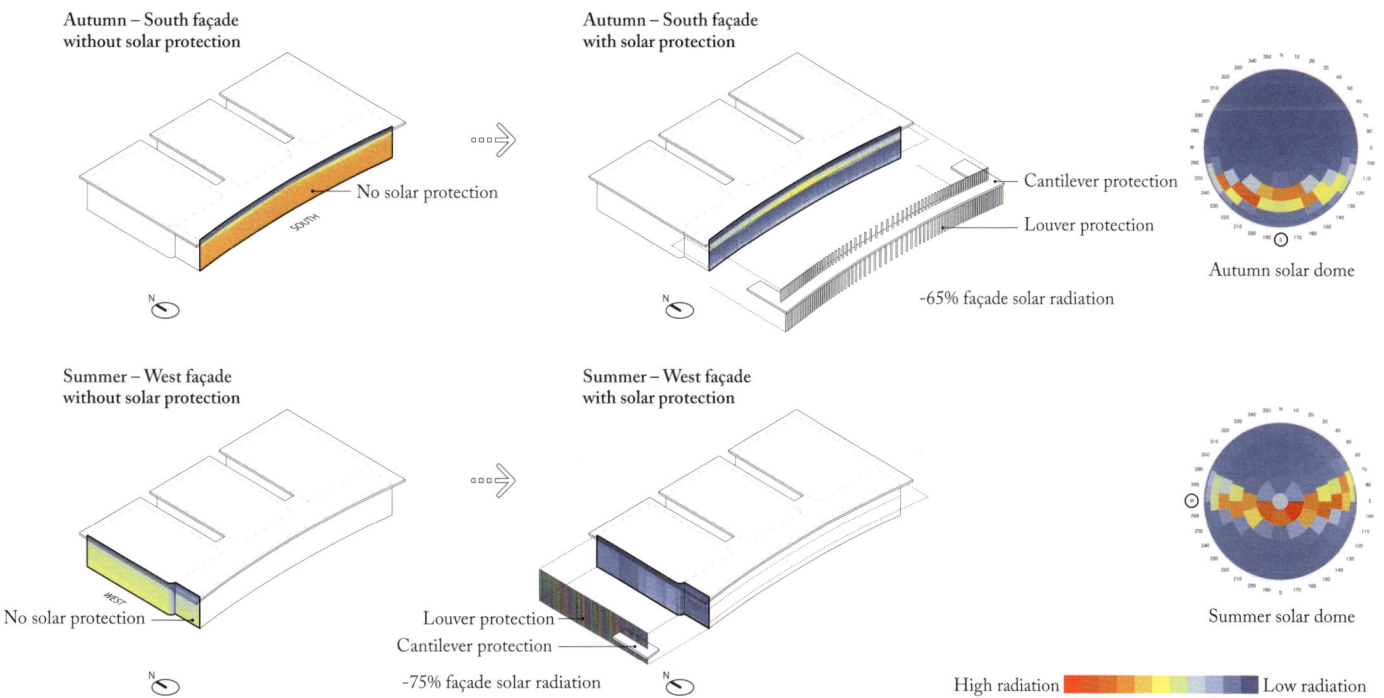

Seasonal solar protection analysis

Buddhist Cultural Center and Dormitory

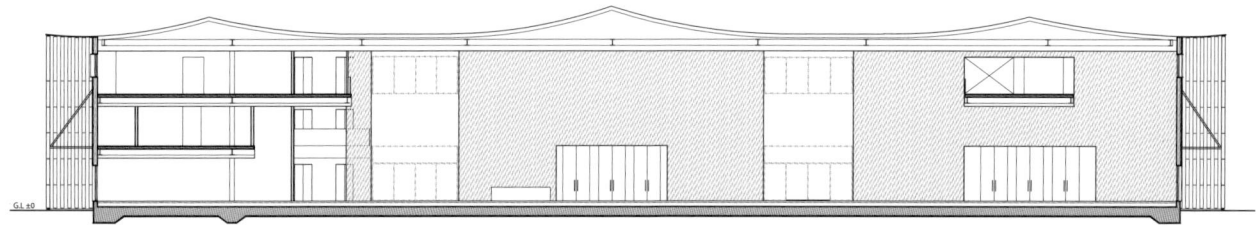

Cultural Center section

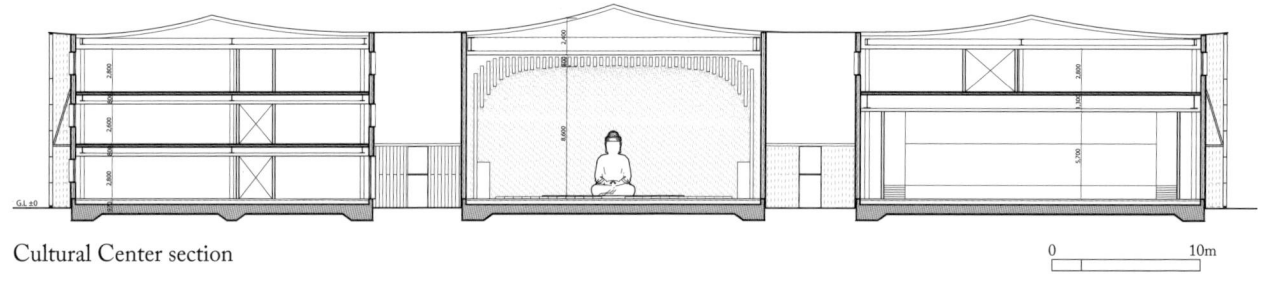

Cultural Center section

Buddhist Cultural Center and Dormitory

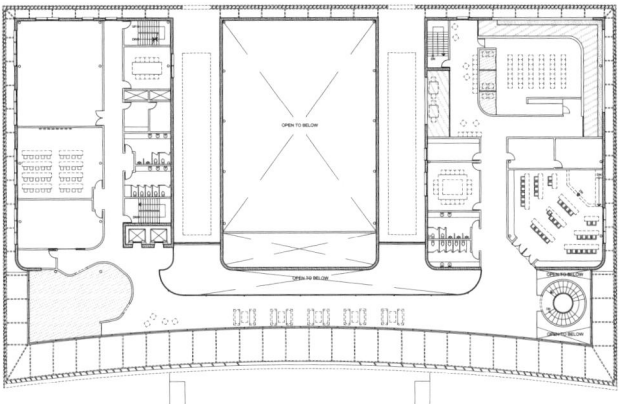

Cultural Center second-floor plan

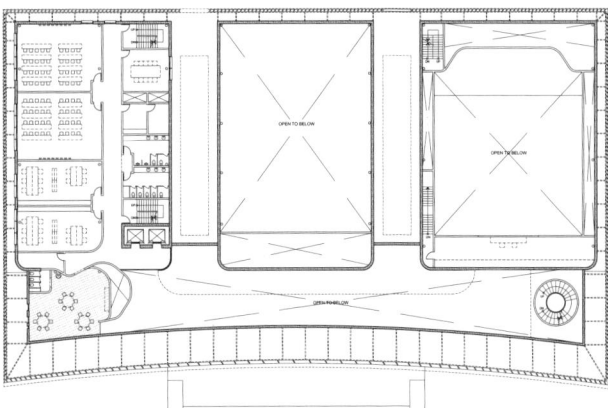

Cultural Center first-floor plan

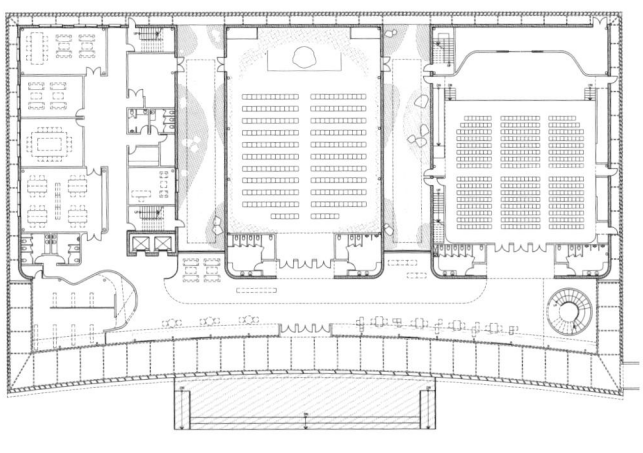

Cultural Center ground-floor plan

Buddhist Cultural Center and Dormitory

Buddhist Cultural Center and Dormitory

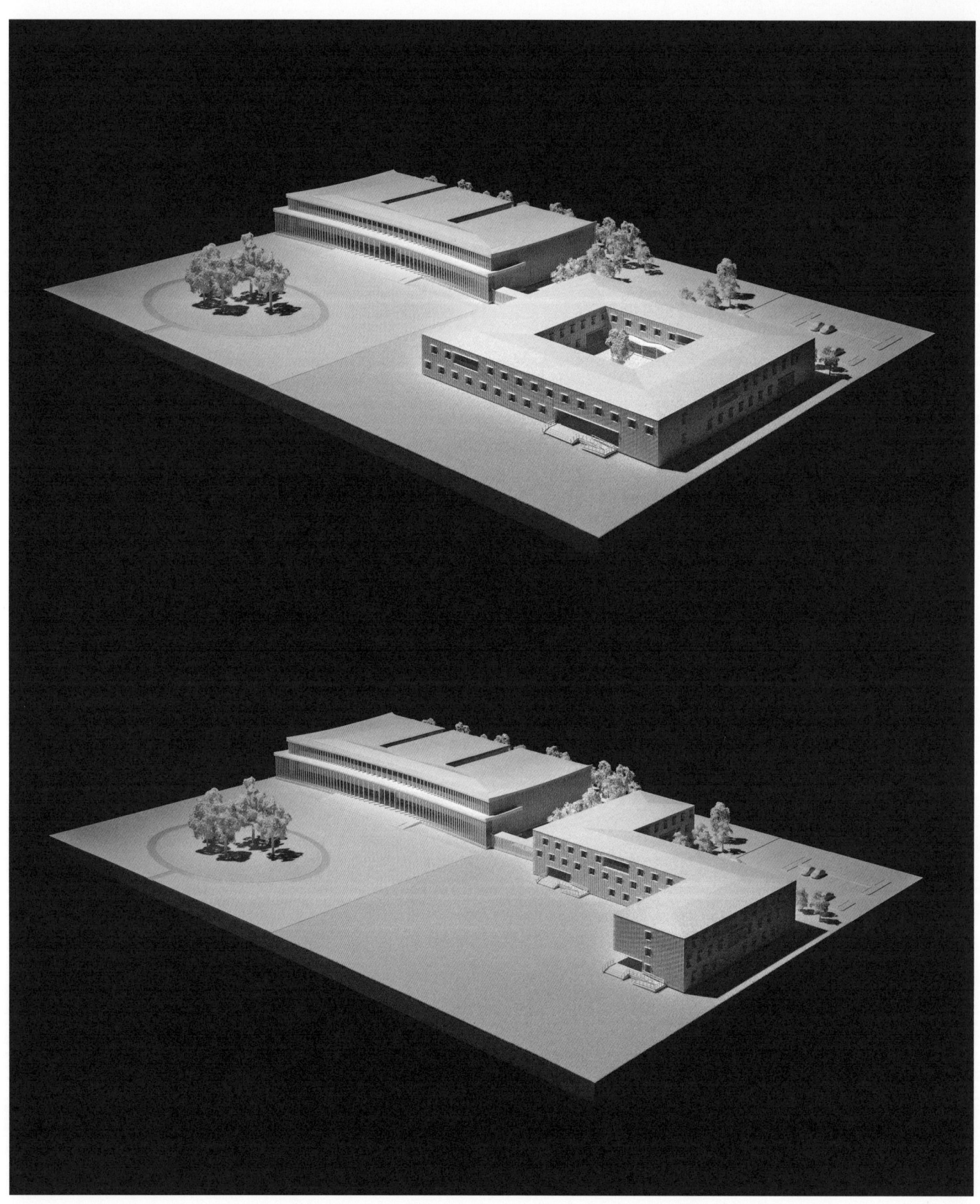

Buddhist Cultural Center and Dormitory

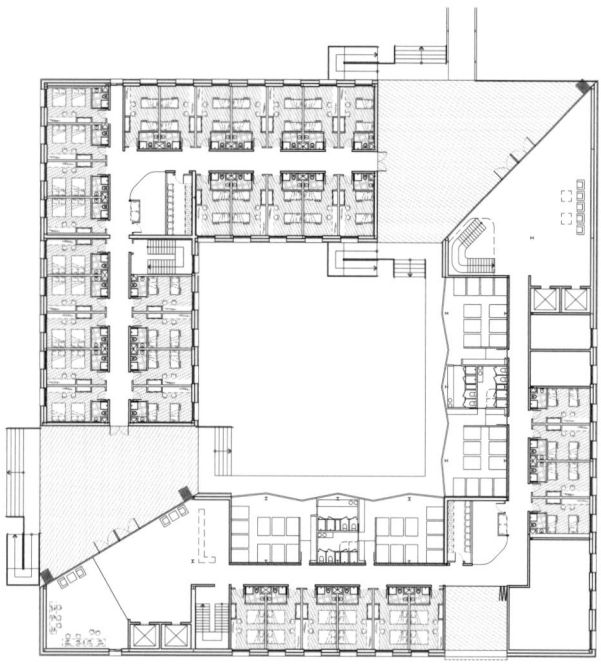

Dormitory ground-floor plan scheme 1

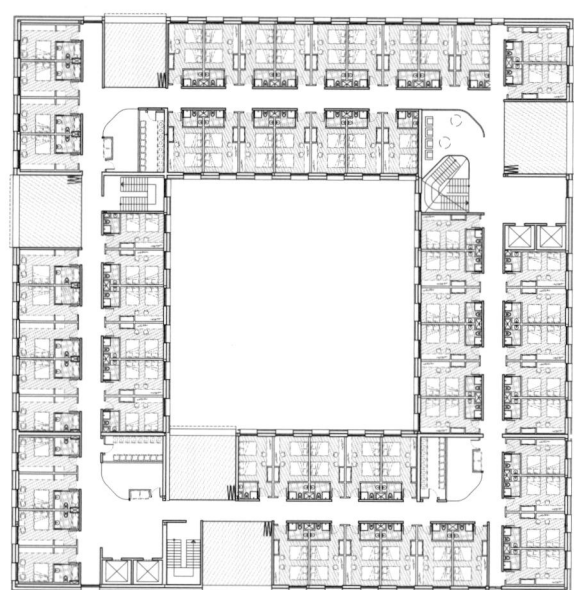

Dormitory first-floor plan scheme 1

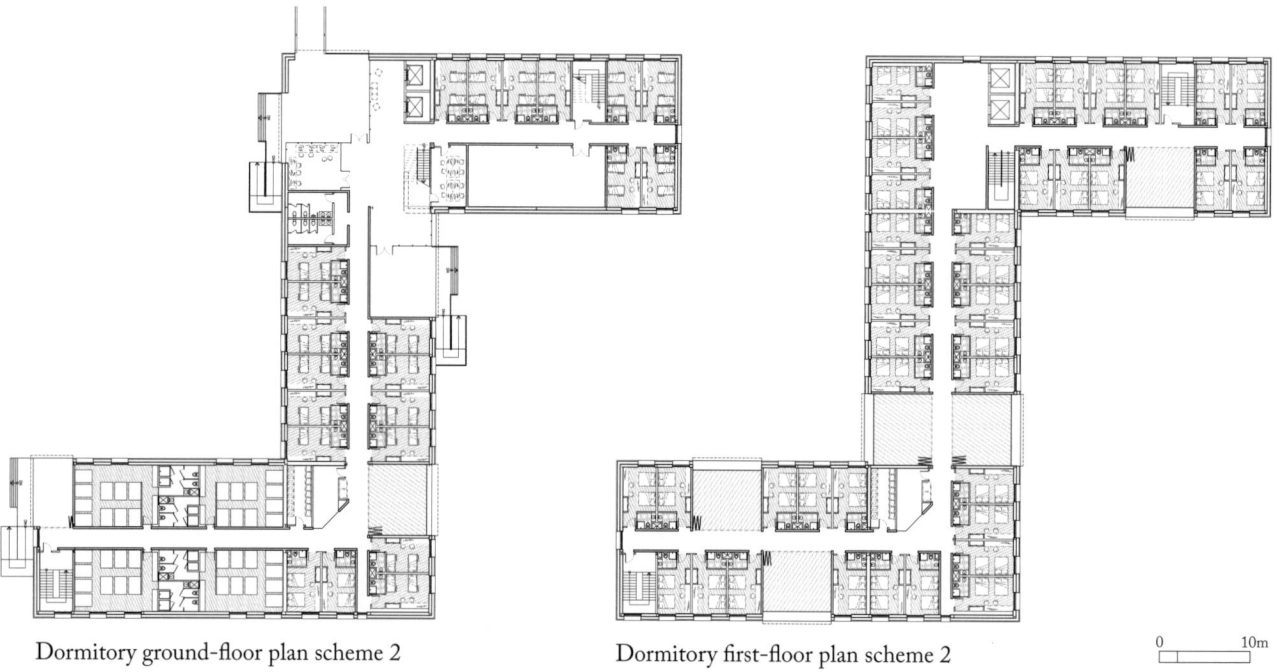

Dormitory ground-floor plan scheme 2

Dormitory first-floor plan scheme 2

Buddhist Cultural Center and Dormitory

MILAN EXPO—
WORLD CRISIS

Challenge our notions of agriculture through architecture, and of architecture through the pavilion's multilayered sustainable strategies

Milan, Italy | 2014

passive solar controlled sustainable structure built w/ local scafolding system for later dismantling & reuse in agriculture.

Milano Expo

At the current rate of ever-increasing urban density, with more than half of the world's population living in urban centers, traditional farming will become less sustainable as the way to feed our cities. The prospect of urban farming has been gaining traction, with food needing to be produced and distributed locally to avoid what is traditionally an increasingly wasteful transportation system.

The 2015 Korean Pavilion at the World Expo held in Milan would illustrate possibilities and ideas for urban farming and sharing, and it would challenge our notions of agriculture through its architecture, and of architecture through the pavilion's multilayered sustainable strategies.

Built with a mix of low- and hi-tech materials, the pavilion would be entirely recyclable to minimize the waste left by our participation at the Expo; it would stand as an educational construction, emphasizing through its architecture our significant commitment to designing for a shared and less wasteful environment.

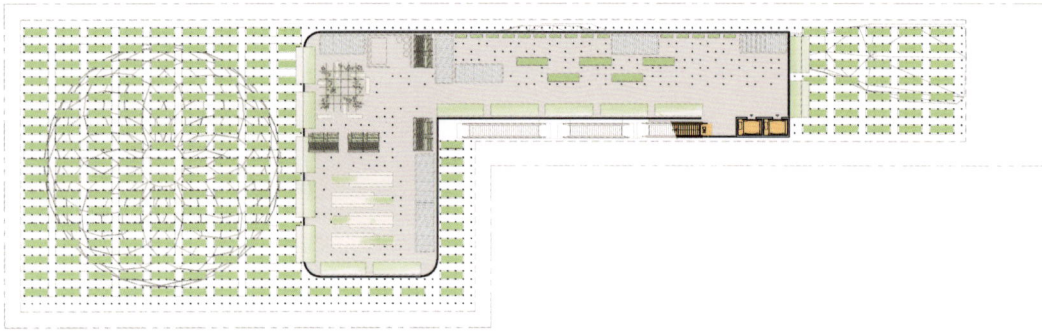
Roof plan

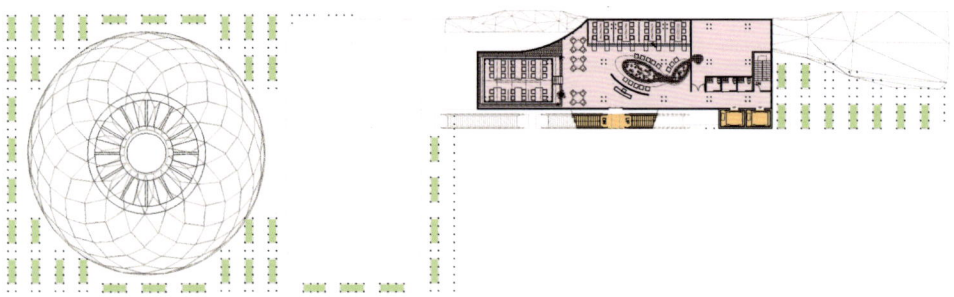
Second-floor plan

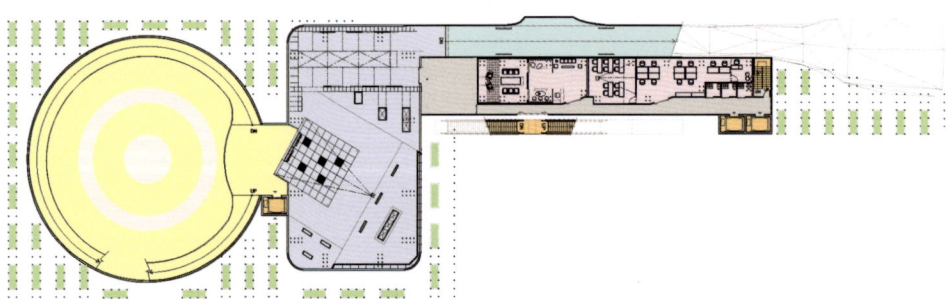
First-floor plan

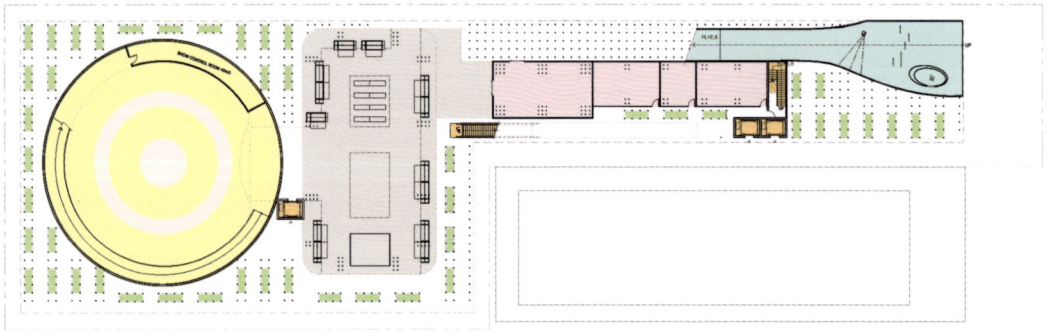
Ground-floor plan

Milan Expo—World Crisis

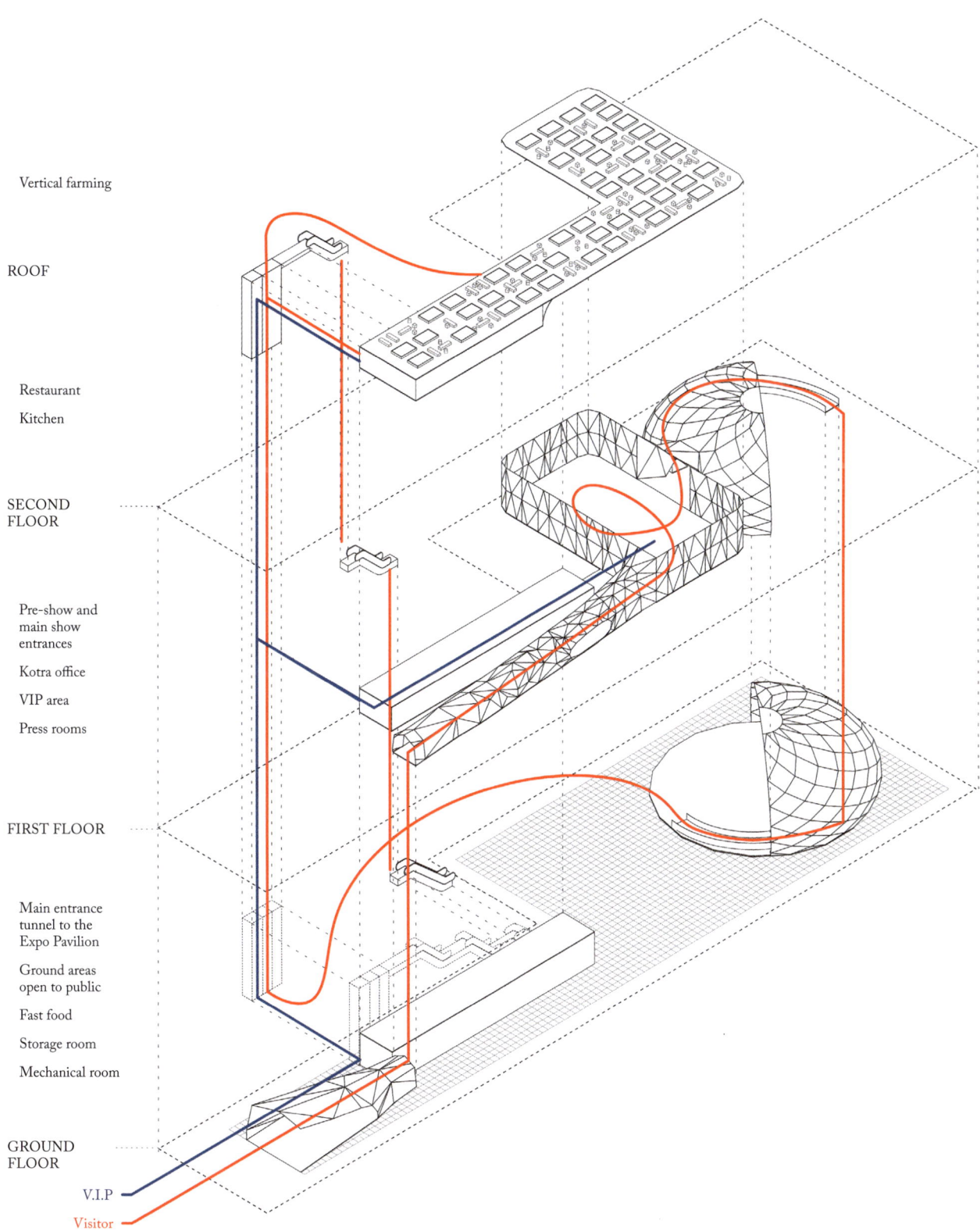

Circulation diagram

Milan Expo—World Crisis

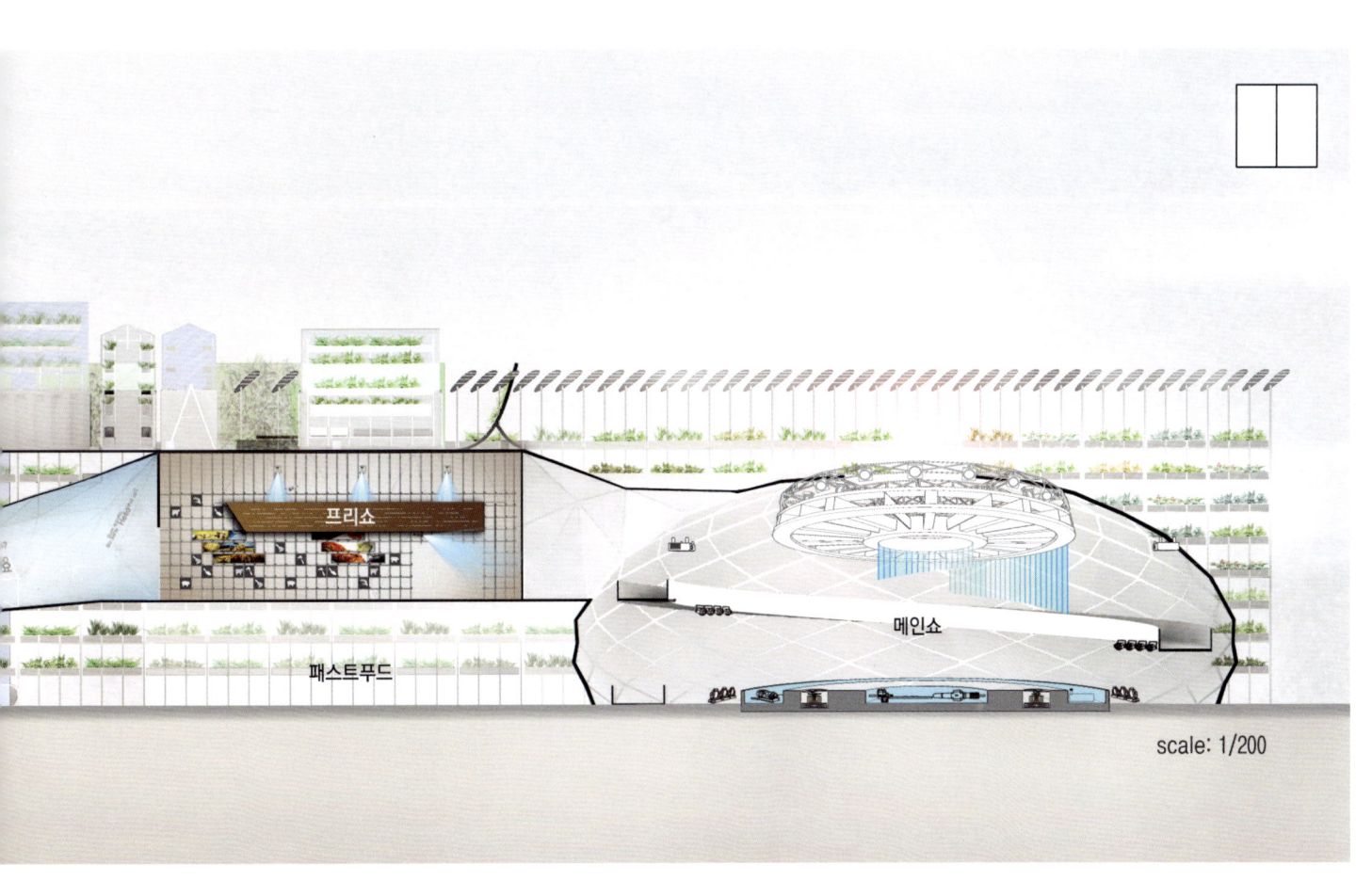

scale: 1/200

The primary building material is a locally manufactured scaffolding system, commonly used for building maintenance and construction, which minimizes pollution due to low-mile transportation and, thanks to its flexibility, is easily assembled and taken apart once the Expo ran its course, and to serve other purposes.

The pavilion's scaffolding system serves the dual purpose of structurally supporting the building in the form of a three-dimensional frame for the space. Occupying the entirety of the site, it was conceptually thought of as a continuous and dense urban farm, from which all required exhibition spaces are carved out as negative voids.

On the roof, the dense three-dimensional mesh of scaffolding turns into a garden, a forest of vertical pipes shaded by leaf-shaped solar panels, generating energy for the building, while shading the crowds of people from the sun's harshest rays during the course of the day.

Milan Expo—World Crisis

Milan Expo—World Crisis

This system—nominally a long entrance ramp, exhibition spaces, restaurants, and a plaza—was designed so that the frame and panels can be reassembled as well, in conjunction with the scaffolding, as greenhouses.

With regard to the heating and cooling strategy, the double-skin membrane structures allow the air to flow through the space inside the skin, naturally ventilating the interior space. Solar panels and plant pots assist with cooling by functioning as sun-shadings. Geothermal heat exchangers enable the building to save energy for both heating and cooling.

In this manner, our pavilion would be feeding the planet twice: once during the Expo in Milan, and once again when it would be reinstalled in the form of greenhouses (using the scaffolding system), the cladding panels, and the planter devices that we designed.

LOUIS VUITTON MAISON SEOUL

Nature vs materiality, and craftmanship and construction through stripes and distortion

Seoul, Korea | 2011

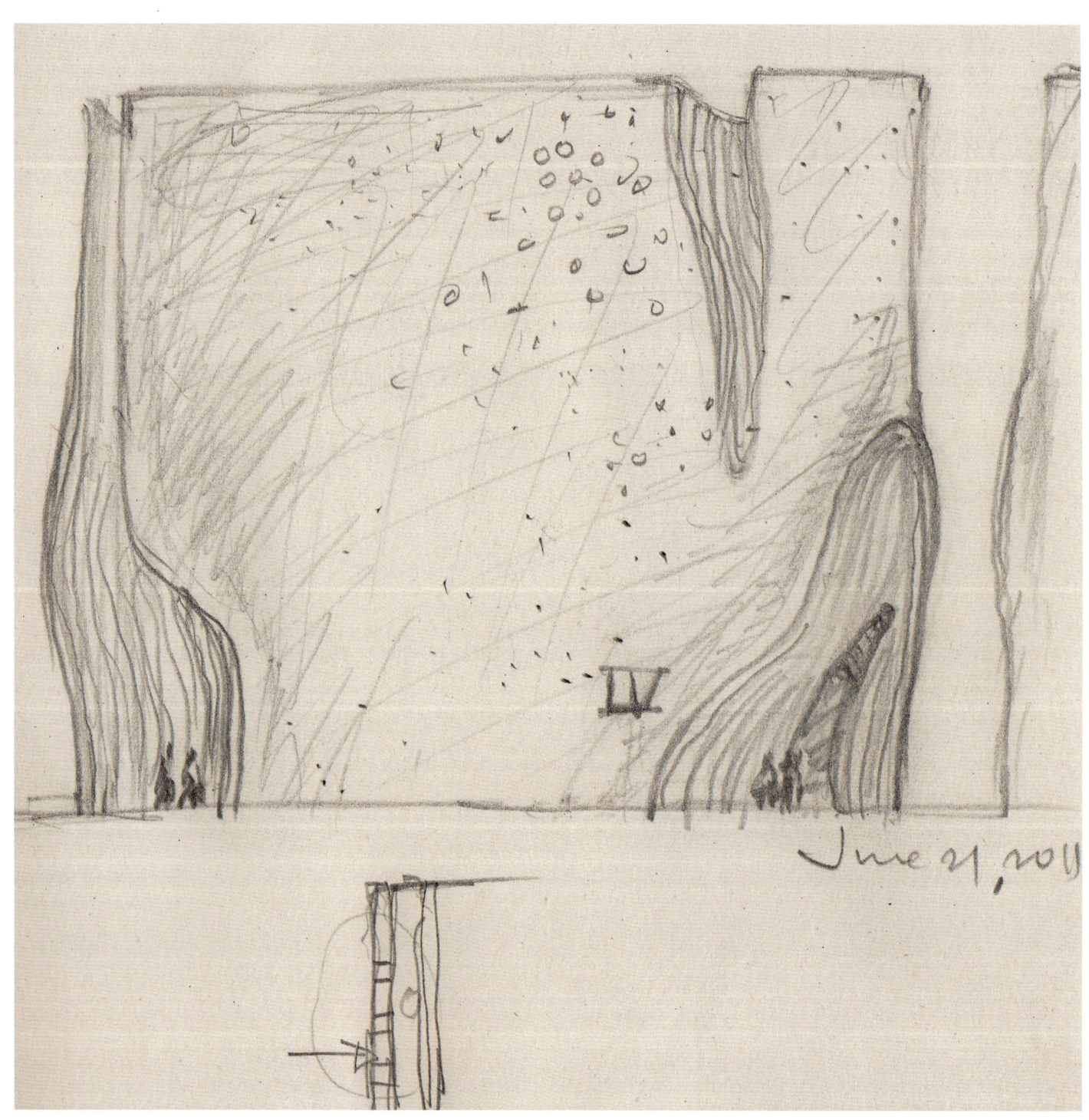

Louis Vuitton Maison Seoul

The focus of this proposal was to fulfill the maximum allowed area into a square building form with a glass façade, which would face the city of Seoul with an oscillating presence. The urban character of the area is rigid, and largely opaque with many other fashion stores. The neighboring buildings did not allow any pedestrians or passersby any glimpse into the secluded buildings. The Seoul flagship store would become a location where the people in the city could pause in fascination at the ever-changing play of light, glass, and stainless-steel mesh, and the journeys ahead at the house of Louis Vuitton.

The form of the façade was to be a series of continuous concave and convex curvatures with slight angles that would diffract light with consistently changing distortions. These would create almost cinematographic perspectives that would highlight the Louis Vuitton collection and ever-changing line of fashion, art, and travel items. These differing geometries generate facetted reflections, which enable viewers, both inside and outside the building, to see constantly changing pictures of Louis Vuitton products, the city, and themselves.

The stripes of the Louis Vuitton line were to be used as a form of brand identification. The stripes used here are subtle and permeable. Natural light is diffused through the stainless-steel mesh stripes within a triple glazing system. The striped screening system would be a welcome contrast to the existing site condition.

Louis Vuitton Maison Seoul

Louis Vuitton Maison Seoul

Louis Vuitton Maison Seoul

Opposite: Street view study, model, 3D print
Below: Section study, model, 3D print

Integrated with the stepped arrangement of the show floors, the users of the building would have various changing views of the urban context. Two concrete masses provide enclaves for entry and rest with a small public park. The building is punctured with a light and air tunnel—Green Tunnel—to allow natural ventilation and provide the retail spaces a unique ambiance for customers.

The Green Tunnel was intended to bring natural light and air through the center of the building. It was to be a steel structure with operable windows for the interior retail and VIP spaces. The Green Tunnel stretches from the café terrace to the entry and can be sealed with translucent fabric in inclement weather. It would also serve as a seasonal display area at the roof level. A small service ladder within the tunnel would allow for maintenance.

Below and opposite: Glass reflection study, model, glass, 3D print

Louis Vuitton Maison Seoul

Louis Vuitton Maison Seoul

The program comprised 10,032 square feet (932 square meters) of internal space in total. The structure was intended to leave all levels column free. The retail space could be subsequently divided and remain flexible for the Louis Vuitton interiors team. The hybrid structure of the building contains two trusses at the third and fifth floors. In conjunction with the cores—three perimeter walls and two 19.7-inch-thick (500-millimeter-thick) concrete retaining walls—the space can be left columnless for the users.

The façade is composed of a combination of molded plate glass and engraved and polished glass. The stainless-steel structure supports the glass and catwalks for maintenance. The thermal envelope is the Okatech triple-glazing system with a steel mesh in between the glass.

GREENSCAPE LIBYA

The goal of carbon neutrality on a regional scale, encompassing cityscape, coastalscape, subscape, and desertscape contexts

Tripoli, Libya | 2011

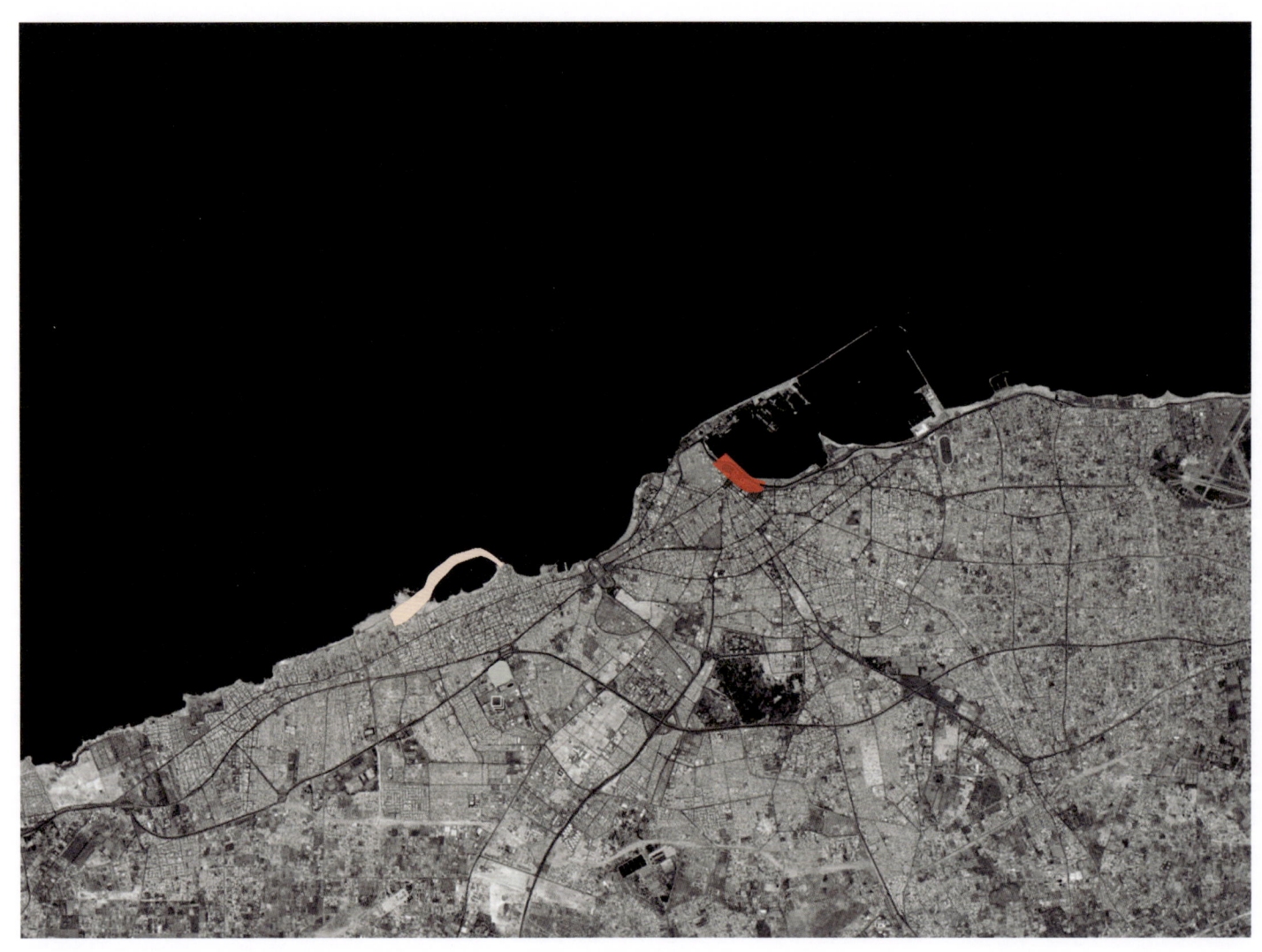

Greenscape Libya

We were developing four key projects in Tripoli that placed an emphasis on sustainable environments, such as renewable power generation, waste management, and recycling facilities, and closed-loop water systems, all with the goal of edging toward carbon neutrality on a regional scale. A further challenge was to establish sustainable industries based on new technologies, including within fishing, organic agriculture, and manufacturing.

The climate throughout most of Libya's coastal lowland is Mediterranean, which features warm summers and mild winters. Rainfall is rare, and the dry climate results in a year-round 98 percent visibility, with average winter temperatures of 59–64.4°F (15–18°C), and summer temperatures of 78.8–84.2°F (26–29°C). With such low levels of rainfall and high winds, the air quality is particularly dry from March to late November.

Greenscape Libya

The Circle Connector is a mixed-use building structure open to various purposes and experiences as a consequence of its unique organizational system. Adopting both horizontal and vertical movement, the Circle Connector seamlessly integrates both public and private spheres of habitation. It creates visual connections around its circular form, while opening itself out to allow views of near and more distant parts of the city and the surrounding natural landscape.

The external form of the Circle Connector is a combination of a circle and needle perforated around the base, allowing movement into and through the central courtyard. The Circle connects the lower six floors in a continuous loop with an external ramp for access to the public landscaped areas of the roof. The three towers align with Mecca while simultaneously providing additional shade to the landscaped circle within.

The Circle Connector is located at a major interchange between the second ring road and three large sports stadiums. It would serve as a landmark, both in terms of the stadia and termination of this large ring road.

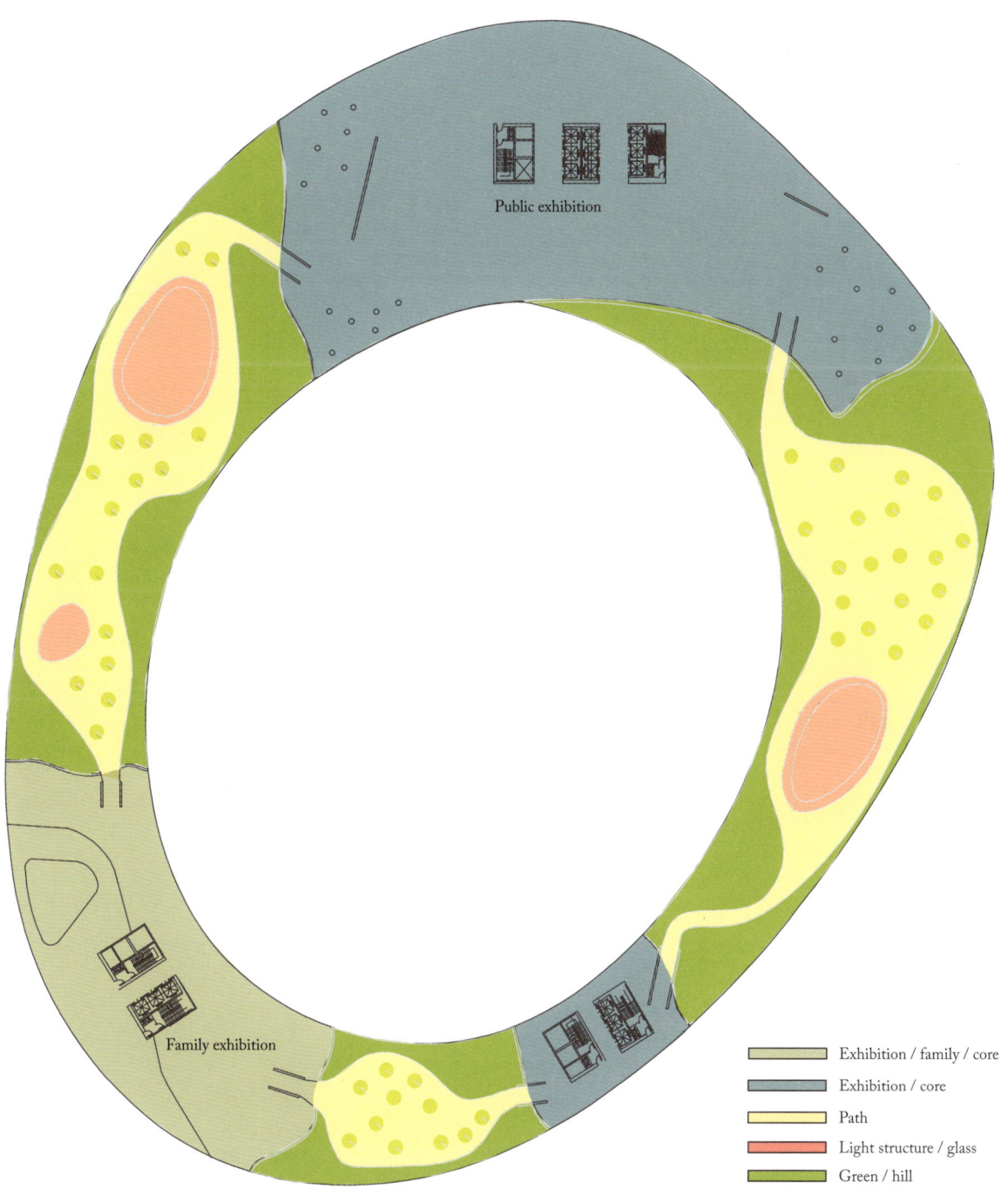

Greenscape Libya

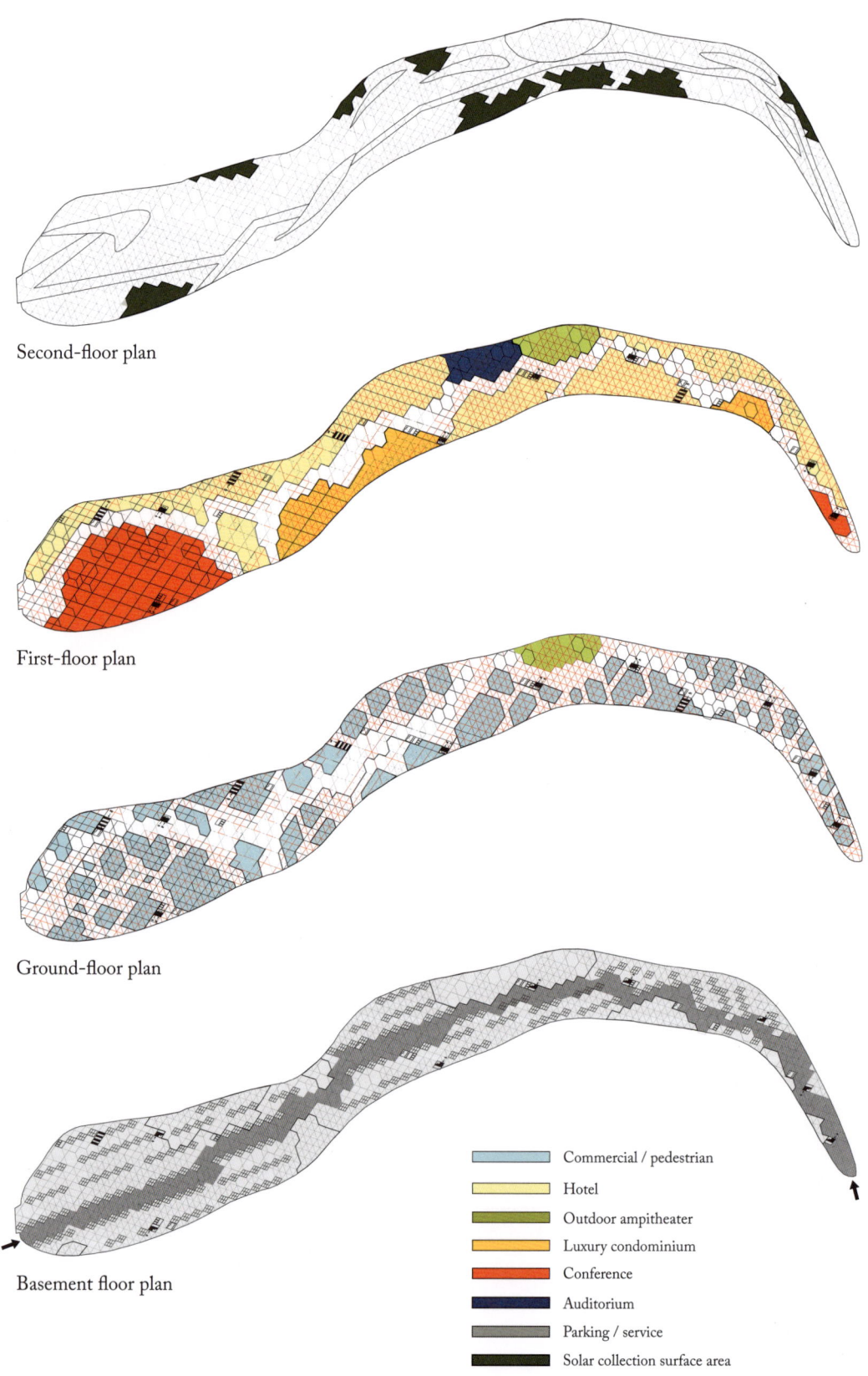

Greenscape Libya

The Sea Mountain is a cultural forum and conference center that extends out from the city's waterfront to encircle a beautiful pre-existing rocky bay. Its architecture was conceived as a rolling dunescape of multiple functions that stretch along its length to accommodate visitors and locals alike. It is a mega-truss that rolls in three dimensions along an untouched section of coastline in Tripoli. There will be a wide array of public and private spaces made available here, all differing in character and scale.

The entire form emerges tentatively from the sandy shore and up and over the bay, permitting visual access to both the Mediterranean Sea and back across the mainland. The megastructure will lift out of the water to allow boats and vessels to pass beneath as well as to maintain a small footprint in the sea.

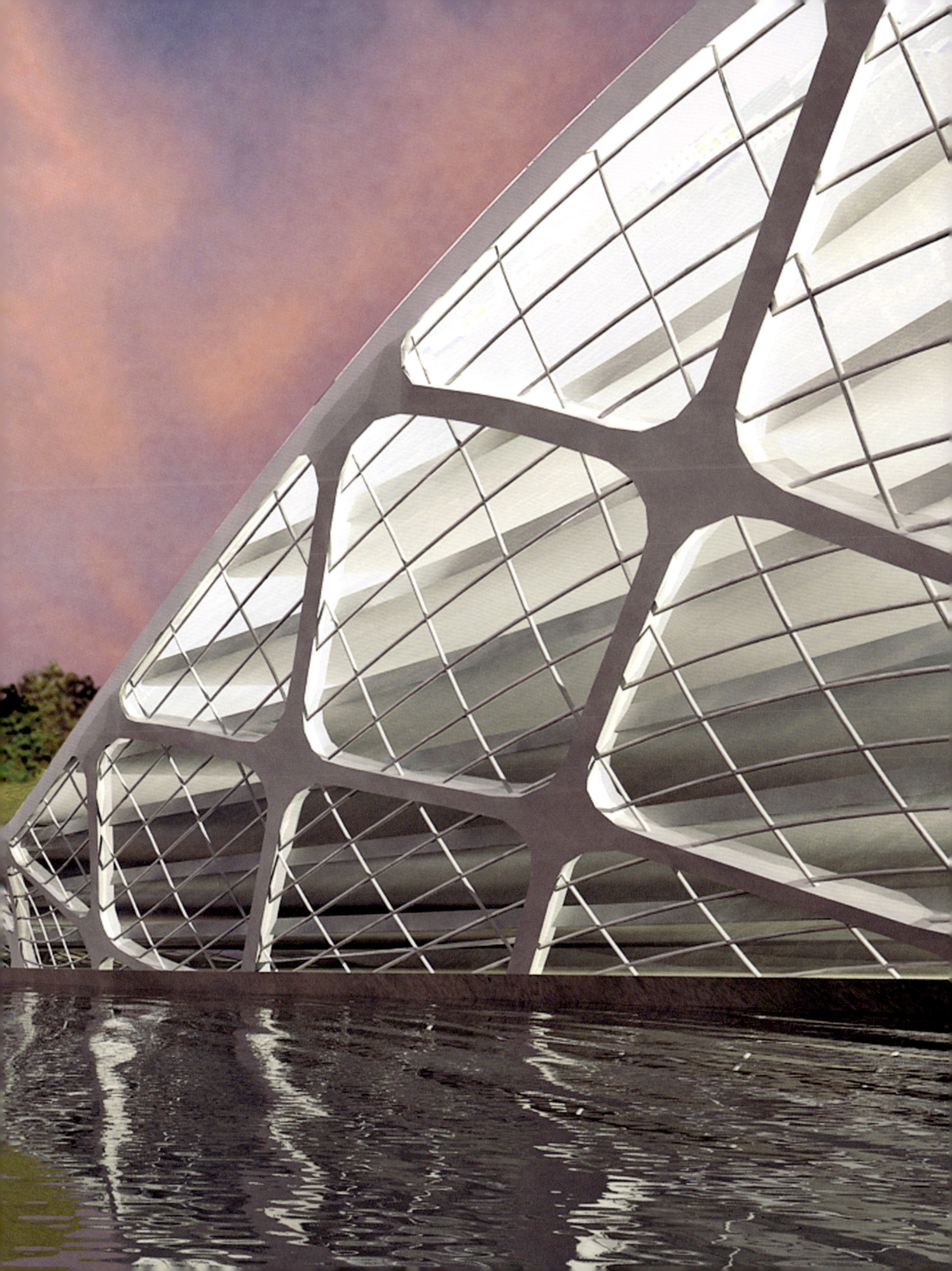

The project aims to become self-sustaining by drawing upon tidal and solar energy. The conditions presented by the southern Mediterranean climate will be harnessed to maintain a low-energy footprint while providing energy for a 450-suite, five-star hotel, a 4,600-seat auditorium, an outdoor amphitheater, a 2,200-seat multipurpose hall, and a cultural strip of small shops for local artists and vendors. Restaurants and cafés will be dotted along the pedestrian walkway with ample public facilities. All of these services will be serviced by a ring road that will connect both ends of Sea Mountain to the existing primary roads. Rainwater will be collected and reused to hydrate the vegetation and plant life, which cover the majority of the surface area of Sea Mountain. Photovoltaic panels will be mounted between mounds of grass to collect solar energy without disturbing the magnificent views of the Mediterranean.

Greenscape Libya

Greenscape Libya

The Red Castle Harbor Restoration project intends to re-establish the strong connection between the Old City of Tripoli with the harbor. The initiative to infill the harbor in the 1970s, leaving it as we experience it today, has long inhibited easy access from the park to the promenade. The restoration will lower the neighboring six-lane road to allow flow out to the harbor's edge. The harbor restoration will include the construction of the Museum of Libya, housing cultural artifacts from all historical and contemporary periods and contexts, commercial and retail spaces, and 700 subterranean parking spaces.

The park has several connected concave areas with spaces for recreation, entrances to the facilities below, a water fountain, and two large square plazas connecting all underground levels to the sky. An open-air souk will occupy the basement level, which is open to four large triangular voids. Local vendors will sell their goods in the shadow of the most valued artifacts detailing Libya's past. The Red Castle Harbor Restoration will bring new life to the historical center of Tripoli and to Libya.

Greenscape Libya

DANA POINT HOTEL

Designing variations to the site's elevated plateau and providing a rhythm with the topography and nearby ocean

Dana Point, California, United States | 2014

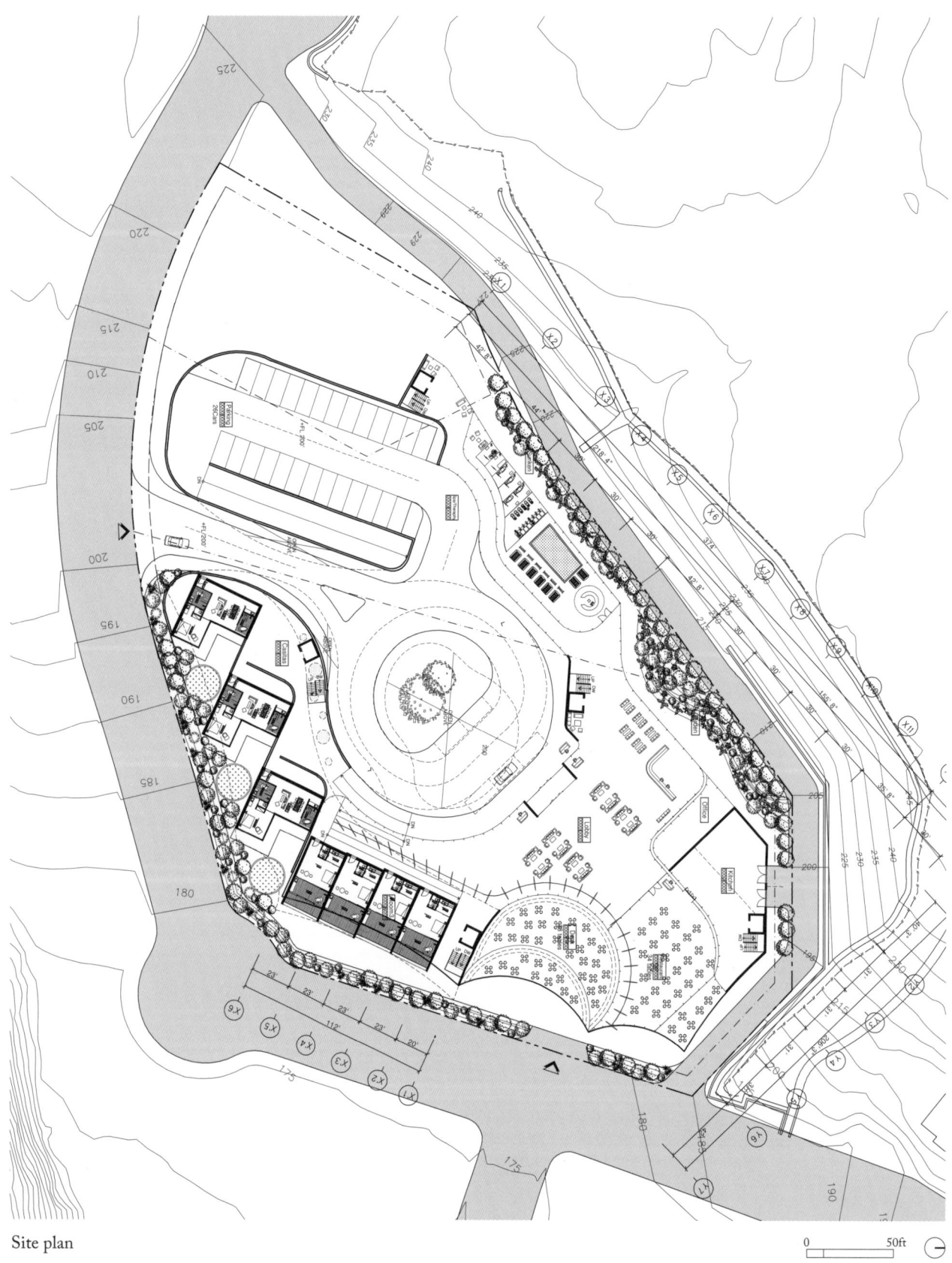

Site plan

Dana Point Hotel

This commercial residential site is in Dana Point, a famous area known for its exceptionally beautiful views of the Pacific Ocean. There is an elevation difference of about 99 feet (30 meters) between the right and left sections of the site. The hotel's residential area starts at the apex of the hilltop site and takes in the sweeping views of a green plane toward the Pacific Ocean, which opens out beyond.

This project required a wide range of programs, including various types of hotel rooms—the client wanted all rooms to have ocean views—and for it to also accommodate the maximum number of rooms allowed, a hotel lobby, parking facilities, the coherent planning of vehicle circulation from the site entrance to the parking lot outside the hotel lobby, a public garden, and numerous other hotel facilities.

The design follows a contour line across the site, charting a logical circulation plan that delivers ocean views to all rooms. There is a height limit at the highest point on the site; the scheme, however, accommodates the maximum number of general-sized rooms possible.

Dana Point Hotel

Dana Point Hotel

Due to the difference in elevation on the site, the project placed a significant emphasis on an accessible entry route for vehicles and for onward circulation. Moreover, the circulation at the entrance to the site and on to the hotel lobby is where visitors form their first impression of the hotel, so we opted for a large sunken space to accommodate vehicle circulation. The entrance begins at the lowest point of the site. From the bottom of this sunken terrain, when a vehicle arrives at the hotel lobby, it approaches by following the site's outer lines to enter the underground parking lot. The varied elevation levels of the hotel room building can be seen from the bottom of the sunken area. By arranging the layout of the building to follow the form of an organic curve, however, it could conform to the quirks of the topography while also preventing the building from appearing monumetal or imposing.

Dana Point Hotel

The primary asset of this hillside location is, of course, its wide panoramic views of the Pacific Ocean, prefaced by the green public garden plateau leading down to the waterfront. People are able to wander the public garden and take in the breathtaking aspect. In our design, we broadened the public green garden by placing decking where the hotel rooms begin. The upper and lower decking spaces take advantage of this difference in topographic levels, and remain unimpeded by the vehicle circulation around the garden. The decking area provides both a calming space for visitors to take respite when in their rooms and is also a stunning vantage point from which to enjoy the magnificence of California's mighty Pacific Ocean.

Dana Point Hotel

SAMPYO HEADQUARTERS

Changing designs and considerations
for early phase design alternatives

Seoul, Korea | 2020

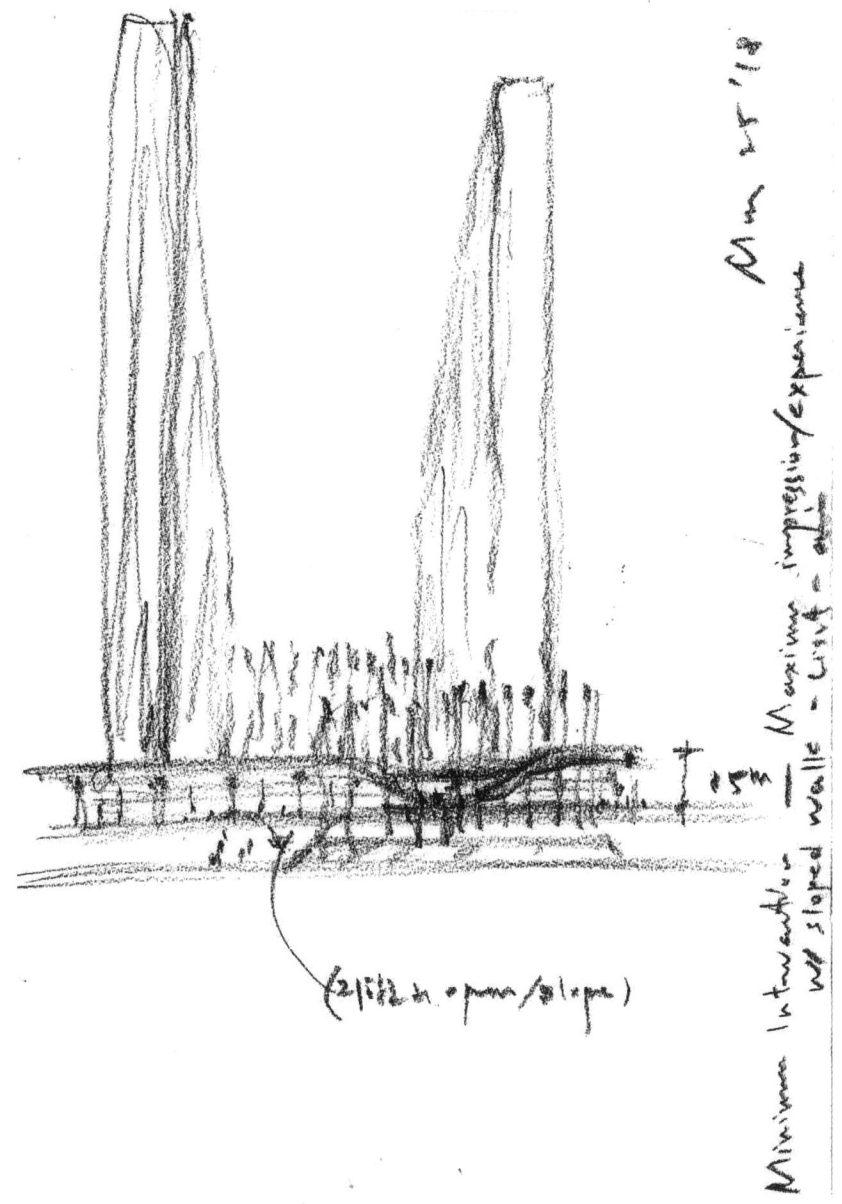

(2/ft2 n. open / slope)

Minimum intervention. Maximum impression/experience
w/ sloped walls - light - etc.

Mm 25 '10

Sampyo Headquarters

This design was for an office tower for Sampyo, a company well known for producing cement and who was broadening its business to include precast concrete. The client wanted to build a headquarter office tower, or an "officetel" tower (similar to studio-type housing) with commercial facilities for the lower levels. The proposed site is in the northwest part of Seoul, an area being newly developed.

Officetel is an unusual type of residence in Korea that is a combination of housing and office space. This type of architecture has a limitation on floor area so it needs to be a very compact size. In order to maintain decent quality regardless of its compact size, we had developed lots of unit types, such as duplexes. Of course, profitability was one of the biggest considerations of this project, which shouldn't be neglected.

Our first consideration was to lay out two towers as far as possible within the site boundary, with an allowance for wind and air to move freely. This was not only compliant with city guidelines, but also coherent with the site context, which would have a big commercial building right behind soon after the completion of our buildings. We believed this "axis of wind" should also work as a pedestrian axis as well so that pedestrian flow between two commercials could naturally become active and eventually vitalize this area.

We planned to locate the office tower on the east side of the site in order to connect directly to the subway station at the basement level. We next considered how to connect the office with the commercial lower levels. We placed some commercial programs on the lower levels of the tower and made them more permeable from the outside. Precast façade panels, which were initially intended to cover the entire tower, were too rigid for this commercial program. By adding precast column colonnades and an arcade, the lower levels became more approachable for visitors.

Sampyo Headquarters

With this new development site, there was a deficiency of green space. In fact, there is no green space close enough in this neighborhood, thus we decided to provide a pleasant green space to residents, visitors, and commuters of this area. Including a green slope was our best alternative for the commercial lower level in this perspective. Visitors wandering around the commercial levels could reach a green space on every level, providing a place to feel refreshed. In light of the overall lack of greenery across the new northwestern development, this green slope could be the most powerful strength of this project.

Sampyo Headquarters

Sampyo Headquarters

Sampyo planned that the new headquarters tower, with its structure and façade in precast concrete, would act as a showroom to advertise their technology in precast. Collaborating with Sampyo's precast structure engineer, we endeavored to figure out what we could do with current technologies.

After several financial profitability studies on what to build and how much to build, the project was picked up again. However, we did not have much choice as to the numbers in terms of the volume and orientation of each building.

We aimed to achieve a very neat, clean, and rather classic look for the overall façade with precast panels. But immediately the weight of the panels, when applied to a high-rise building, became quite a major issue, and one that demanded resolution. When we provided them with the cost factor analysis, Sampyo had to question if it really was willing to spend a big portion of money only on the façade. And the client's answer was "no." After having strenuously sought out the technical solution of the precast façade, it was abandoned due to the cost, the weight, and its consequent inefficiency, and other issues to do with delivery and assembly. In the end, we ended up developing an aluminum curtain wall façade system.

Sampyo Headquarters

VISANG HEADQUARTERS

Inspired by the site conditions, this project seeks to establish an identity of place within a new urban context and adapt the pre-existing topography

Gwacheon, Gyeonggi Province, Korea | 2020

Space between
where
we dwell
&
rest

AnT 2
활력, 따라 움직임
dynamic/excitent

Visang Headquarters

Gwacheon was established as a satellite city to accommodate government agencies. However, when these agencies gradually moved to Sejong City, the necessity of reinvigorating the Gwacheon economic activity core was raised. The new master plan called "Gwacheon Knowledge Information Town" was launched in response.

This project was to build a headquarters for Visang Education, a rapidly growing educational content producing company. Visang Education planned to lease out about half of the total area, and be able to sell it in the future, which meant that a flexible and homogenous space was required.

The site, accessible via only one road, is characterized by a distinct slope. On one side of the land is a green space. This sloping land situation of the site was an important factor and starting point of the project, making us think that we should make a strong connection with the sloping green area with the main public space.

In our initial studies, the ground-level public space would accommodate diverse public programs, such as a library, and small auditoriums along a charismatic circular ramp. This ramp would gently hover over the existing landscape and create interesting intersections of natural landscape and public spaces.

The lobby, which normally occupies the ground level in most conventional office buildings, was placed instead on the mid-level. Box-like programmatic structures reach out toward the surrounding landscape, affording panoramic views for visitors. These boxes are stacked and rotated, creating free, in-between spaces allocated as outdoor gardens. In effect, nature is not only experienced at a ground level but permeates the buildings in at least three critical areas—the ground level, mid-level, and the rooftop.

Visang Headquarters

Visang Headquarters

Visang Headquarters

As the northern perimeter is sloped, it starts from one vertex and ends at a higher level, which continues to become the buffering green area. We experimented in copying these sloping lines in different directions, and we found very interesting patterns whereby the lines of a vertex repeatedly touch the ground and detach from them, creating slits. This showed a possibility that light could come through these slits and could create an expression of the interior spaces. We discovered that this experimental ground pattern could form an idea of wings from the entrance road, in keeping with the idea of the client. The pre-existing sloping condition of the site naturally flows and becomes one side of the wing, and the continuing lines on the opposite side becomes the other wing of a bird. The line originating from this external site flows into the interior space, forming a kind of Möbius band, when viewed from the main lobby hall. The line goes toward the rear side of the building and merges organically with the surrounding land. And in order to have the most efficient and homogeneous office space, the mass was made as a simple prism volume above the ground, with the central core serving the working spaces. By placing the mass to the west as possible, the expression of the flow of the land in the eastern side with the green area could be more pronounced.

Visang Headquarters

Visang Headquarters

The design of the façade of the building is always an important topic, especially for an office building. In modern architecture, the structure and the façade are completely separable, so the façade could be designed with a maximum degree of freedom. As the construction cost was limited, we devised a functional and purpose-oriented façade at first, using a simple sun-shading device, such as a vertical louver on top of a simple curtain wall system. The client wanted a more prominent representation through the façade, and so we turned to study a double façade. Our first version of the double façade was made of a curtain wall system inside, with vertically folded aluminum perforated panels as a second layer. This screen would allow more diffused light into the inner working space, while creating a varying special visual effect from outside from different angles. However, this double façade design had to be abandoned due to the enormous rise in the construction cost. Considering the limit on the budget and with easy constructability in mind, we eventually developed a simple curtain wall system with an increased wall area, packed with insulation. This functions much better with regard to energy use. Initially we preferred a three-dimensionally volumetric panel façade, rather than a two-dimensional one, as its expression varies according to the viewing angle, and we would have liked to use precast concrete panels to realize that. But this idea of using very heavy material on the façade was already excessive, as precast concrete is in Korea, in general, still prohibitively expensive. In the end, very thin ceramic panels were chosen as the main wall-forming material. We made certain abstract patterns, using four ceramic–width modules.

Visang Headquarters

Visang Headquarters

We found ourselves asking if the Visang Headquarters project responded adequately to the need of creating an identity of a place in the new urban context, and its adaptation onto the pre-existing topography. Many European projects have a strong inclination to construct a consistent urban fabric based on the history by trying to fill out the parts in order to have a sense of a whole. In Korea it is often quite difficult to trace back the history and construct contemporary cities in continuation with tradition, as our history is disconnected from the modern era, and most of the land and sites are deprived of any background. Many such place identities in Korea are traditionally formed from the topography, characterized with undulating mountains or hills, and thus adaption of architecture onto the pre-existing topography was a rather natural inclination for our final design, which awaits its final realization in the near future.

Visang Headquarters

SEUN DISTRICT #4

Organically connecting a building into the intricate nuances within the city's wider urban fabric

Seoul, Korea | 2017

concept
Shaping the "Voids"
Connecting the "Voids"

Strong context
- street 흘러서
- 층고
- 파사드
- existing street system

flow of walk
sequence of events

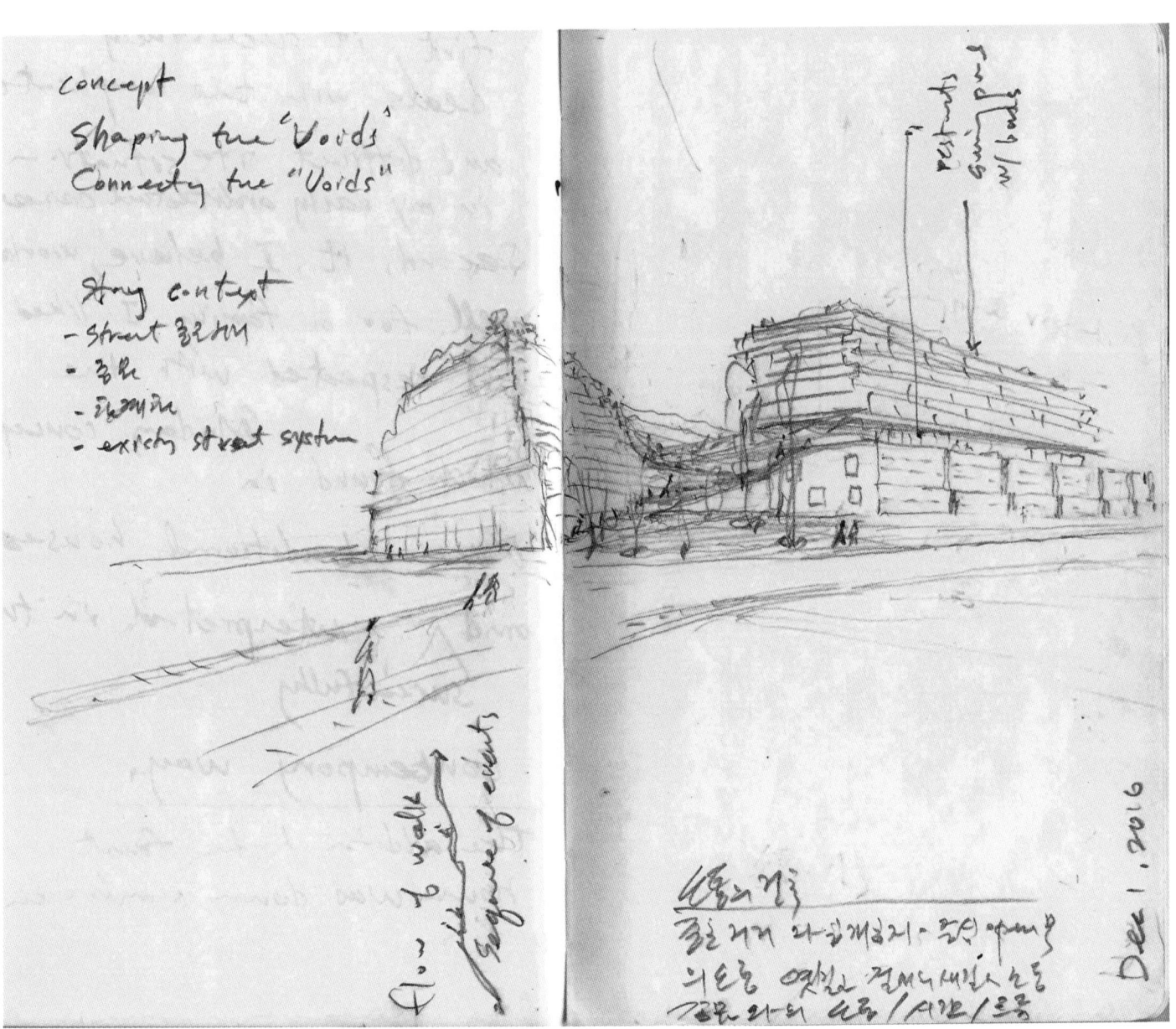

restaurants
w/ swing

산들의 경종
흘러 가게 와의 게출리 - 전신 아래로
의 토들 영상한 절대 세워서 오른
결국 라의 쇼로/시간/흐름

Dec 1, 2016

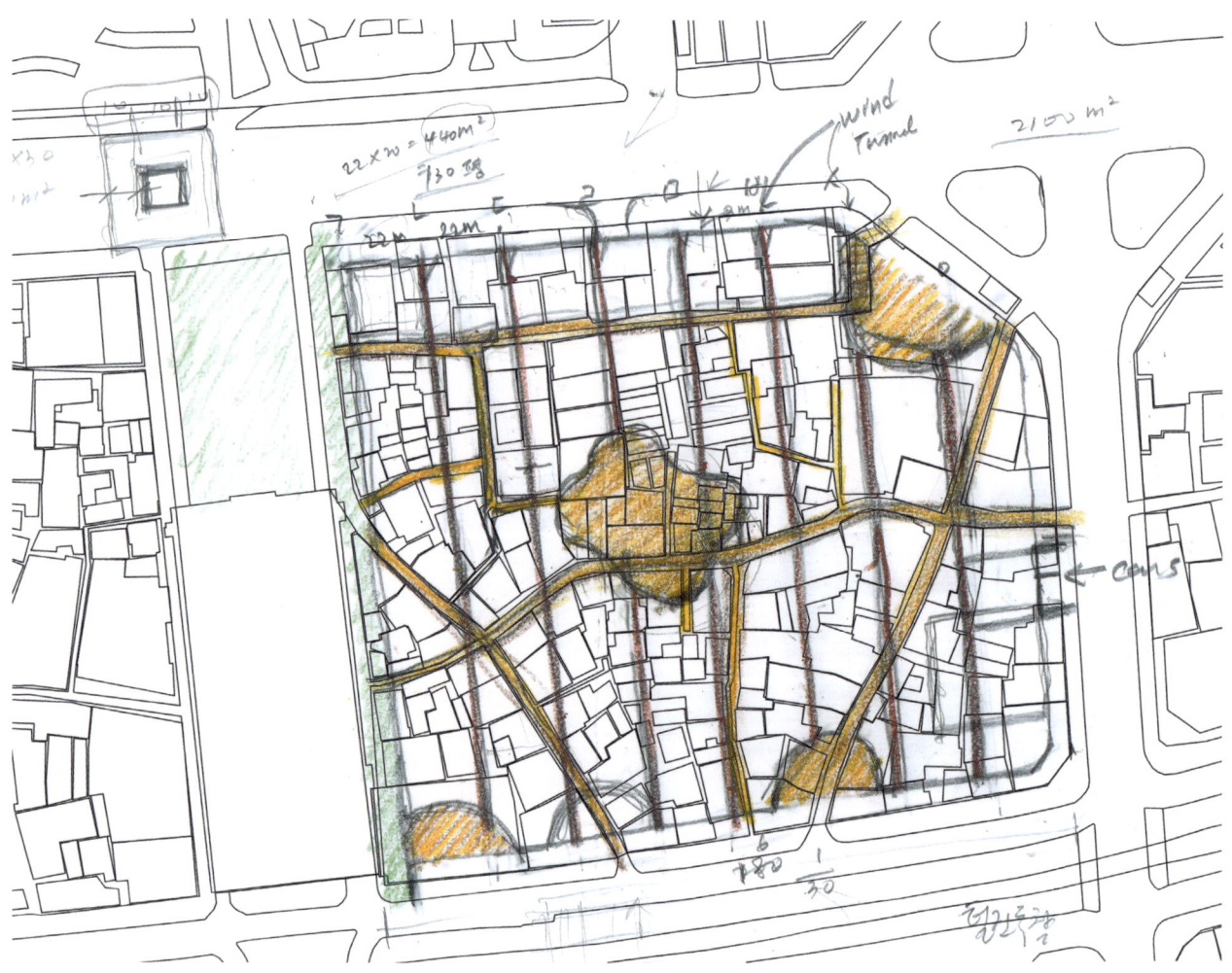

The proposed building is located in the historical Seun district of Seoul, which is surrounded by clusters of low-rise buildings and old alleyways. Just adjacent to the site is a number of significant urban landmarks, such as the Brutalist megastructure, Seun Sanga, and the modern park and river stream, Cheonggeycheon, which stretches through the heart of Seoul. In this context, the project proposed the creation of an urban node that would organically connect to the intricate workings embedded within the wider urban fabric.

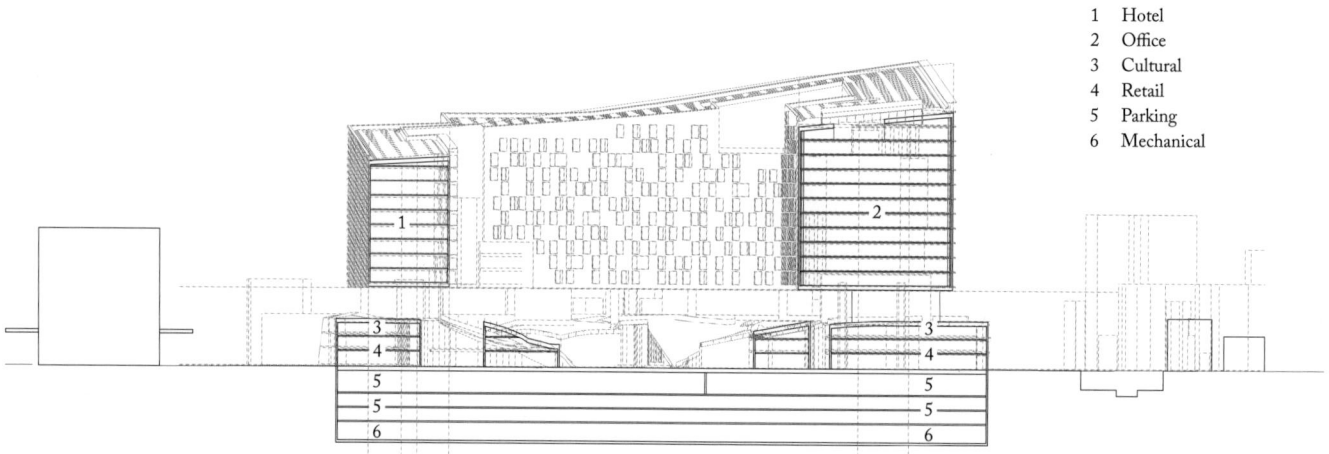

Section

1 Hotel
2 Office
3 Cultural
4 Retail
5 Parking
6 Mechanical

Seun District #4

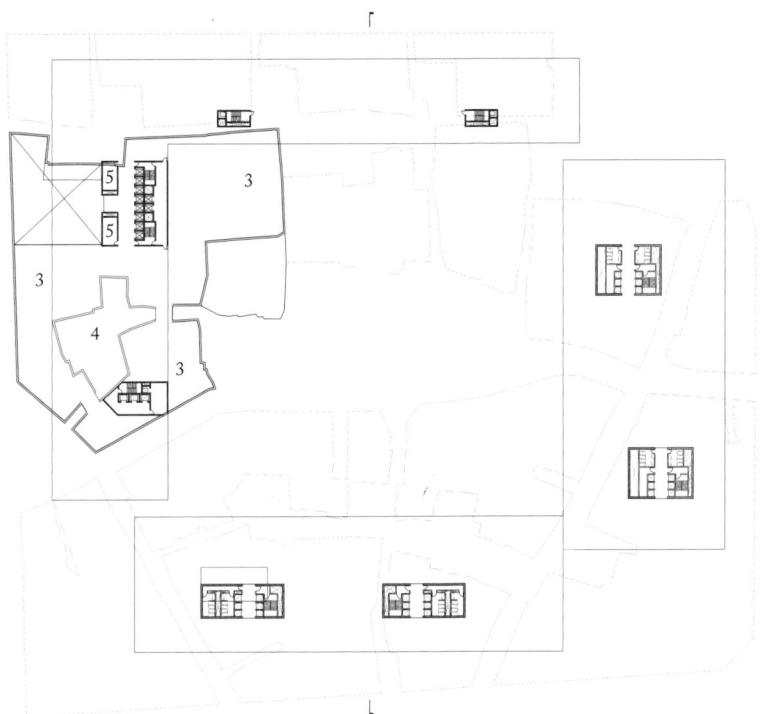

Hotel first-floor plan

Hotel ground-floor plan

1 Reception
2 Lobby
3 Retail
4 Arcade
5 Restroom

0　　30m

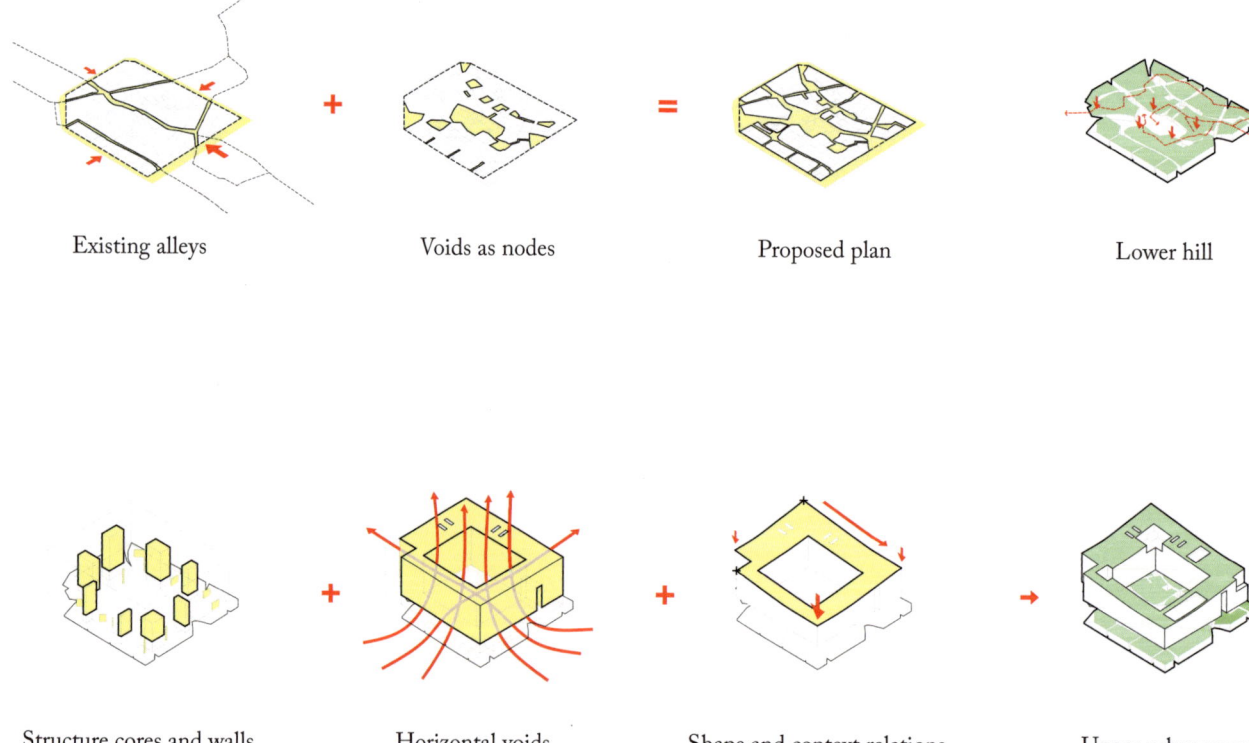

Seun District #4

Architecturally, the project operates around three key urban figures: respectively, the lower-level public podium, the mid-level open landscape, and the floating upper volume, all of which cater to the project's private programs. The form and planning of the ground-level public podium places it in direct juxtaposition with the existing urban context. Drawing the city's old alleyways closer, a wide array of winding streets ultimately converges on the central public plaza, an urban void interpreted as following the traditional Korean courtyard (*madang*). This void acts as a public space in which to host various cultural and commercial events. The plaza naturally connects with the mid-level open landscape that's covered in an expanse of greenery, parkland, and terraces that integrate with the plaza below. The uppermost volume of the project references the courtyard typology of the plan; the upper level is lifted from the ground-level podium to create the narrow slit of a horizontal void, and it offers unhindered panoramic views of the cityscape.

Seun District #4

Seun District #4

The intersection between the building's vertical and horizontal voids also performs the role of an environmental device. The semi-open space, forged in this elevated design, promotes the penetration of air, supplying natural ventilation to the interior. We designed the external façade to follow the form of blocks positioned around a perimeter, with intermittent vertical green walls, thereby reducing solar heat gain and the impact of the varying warmer temperatures of this island climate.

GANA ART CENTER AND VILLAS

Architecture adapts to the environment,
creating a harmonious dwelling

Seoul, Korea | 2019

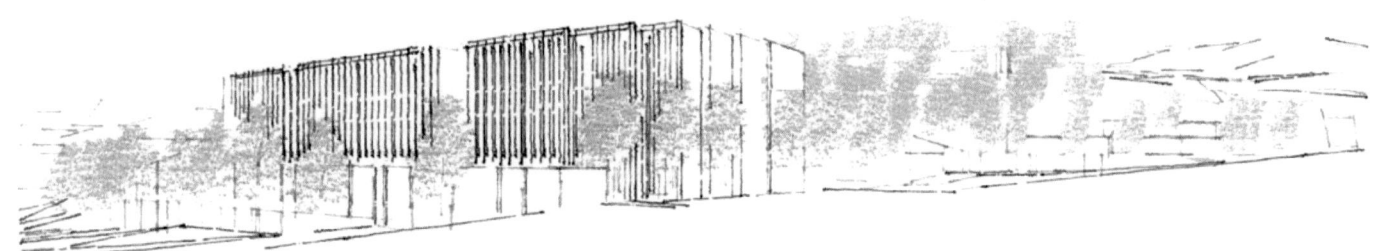

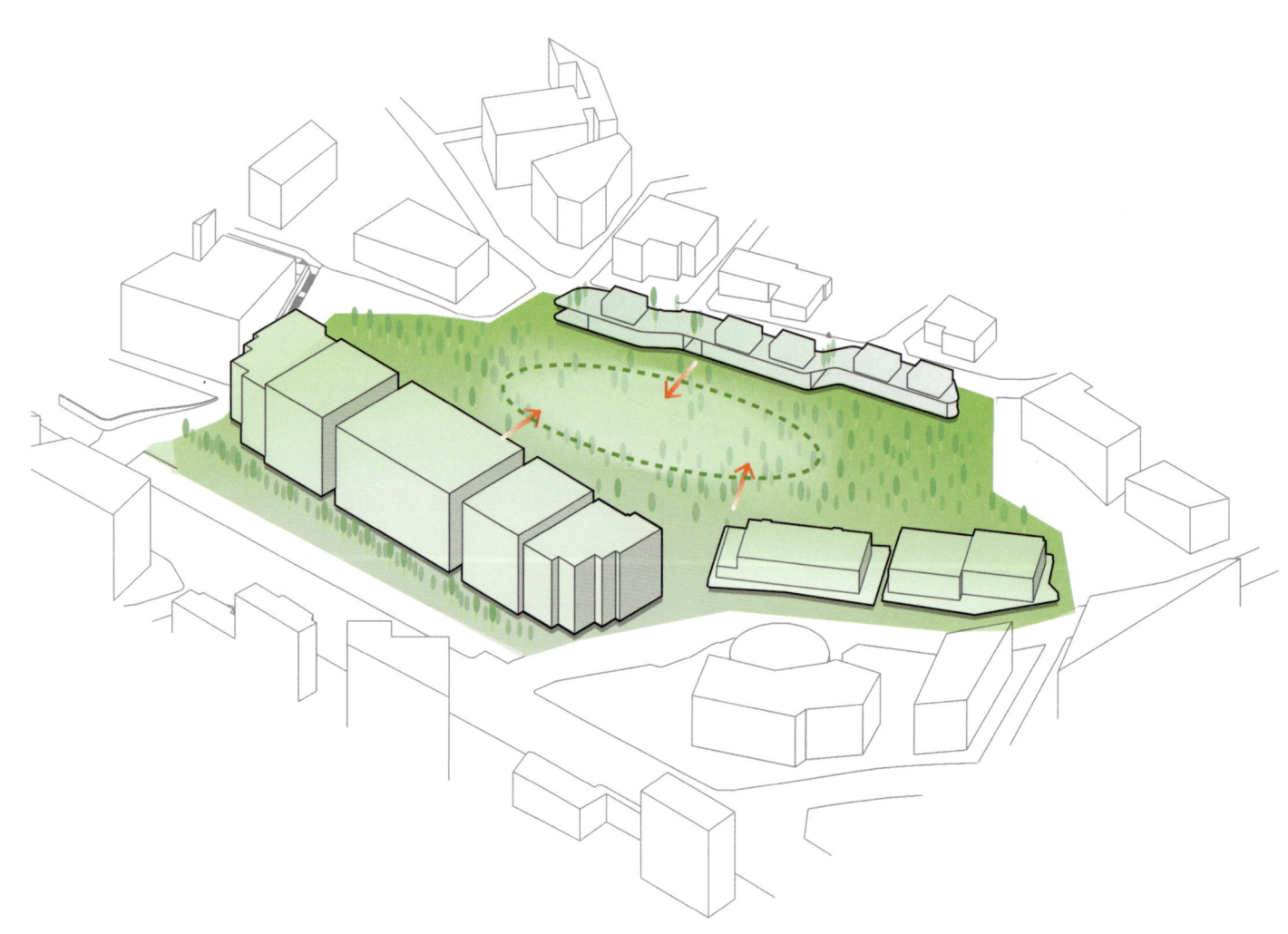

Gana Art Center and Villas

Three residential typologies comprise the proposal for the Pyeongchang-dong Residential Complex. The eighty-unit apartment building sits on the southern frontier of the site, the fifteen-unit multiplex housing toward the northern end, and the four-unit multiplex housing on the eastern border. All three buildings occupy the periphery, loosely demarcating the boundaries of the site and leaving the existing natural landscape in the center intact. While a conventional residential development would have cut away the boulders and the steep rocky terrain for optimum building conditions, in this proposal, architecture adapts to the environment instead. In addition to the unique site planning, the architectural typology of each building is rendered so as to maximize the interaction between the existing natural landscape and architecture. The typologies range from undulating steel plate housings that gently skim the summit of the rock mountain to housing units lifted from the ground by pilotis while being topped with ample rooftop gardens. In all cases, the notion of dwelling is central to the architecture. As Christian Norberg-Schulz exerts, "Man dwells when he can orient himself within and identify himself with an environment, or in short, when he experiences the environment as meaningful. Dwelling therefore implies something more than 'Shelter'."

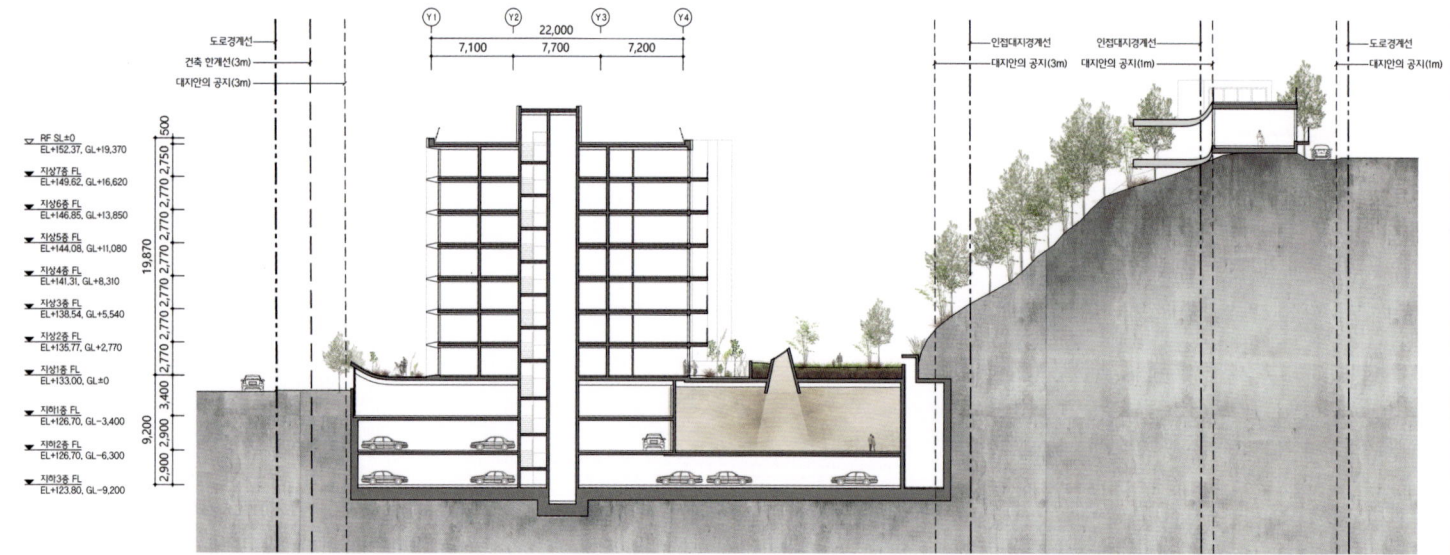

Site section

Gana Art Center and Villas

Gana Art Center and Villas

Gana Art Center and Villas

Gana Art Center and Villas

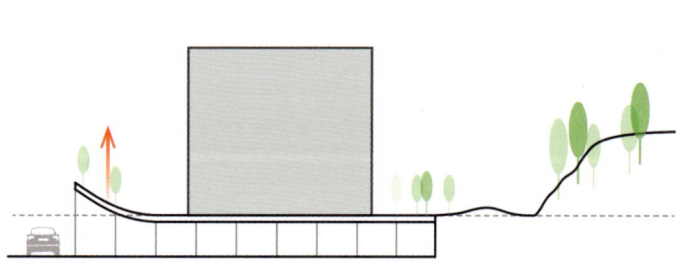
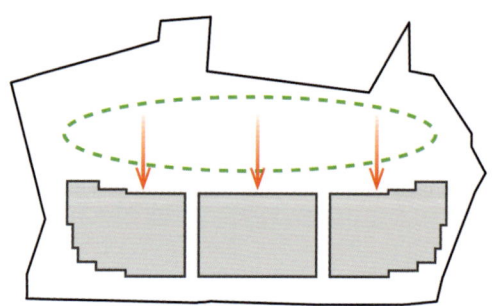
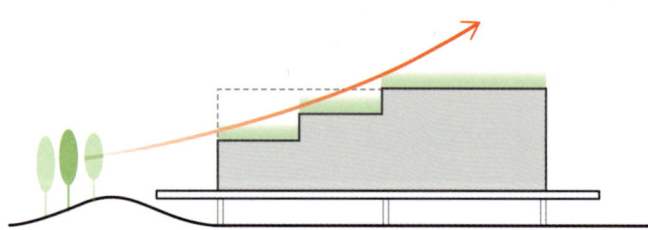
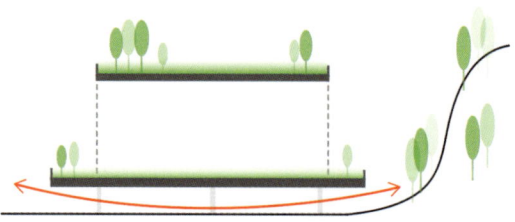
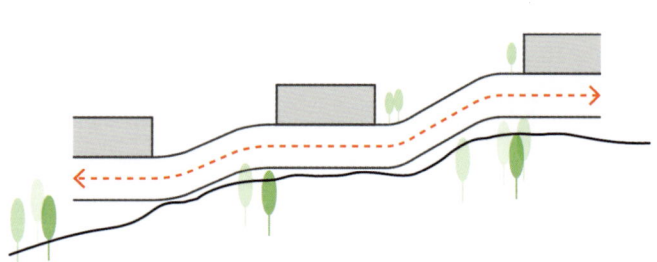
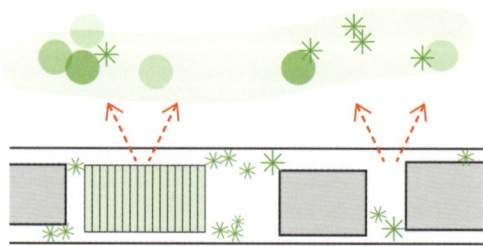

Gana Art Center and Villas

Gana Art Center and Villas

LOS ANGELES COMMUNAL HOUSING

The space has been configured like small houses in a village clustered together

Los Angeles, California, United States | 2017

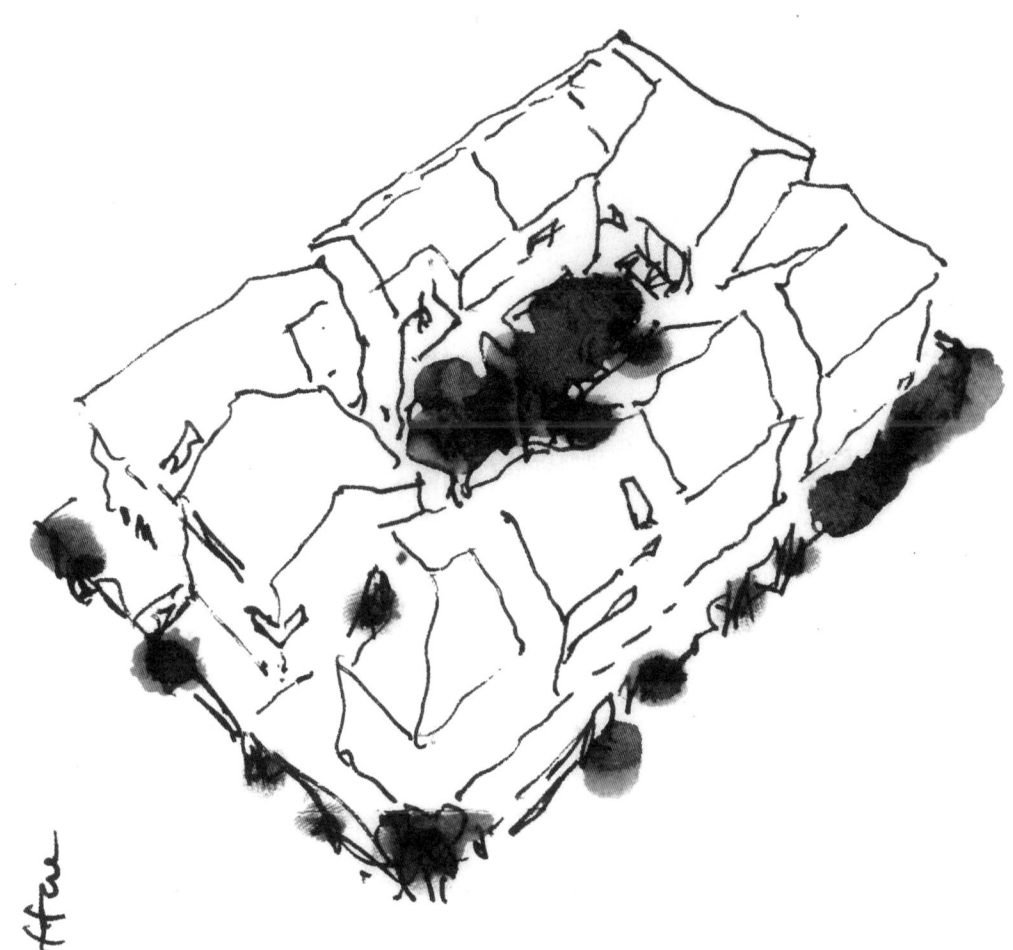

'Commune village'
Housing/cafe/office

Communities sharing the
void in the middle
as garden/gathering
place...

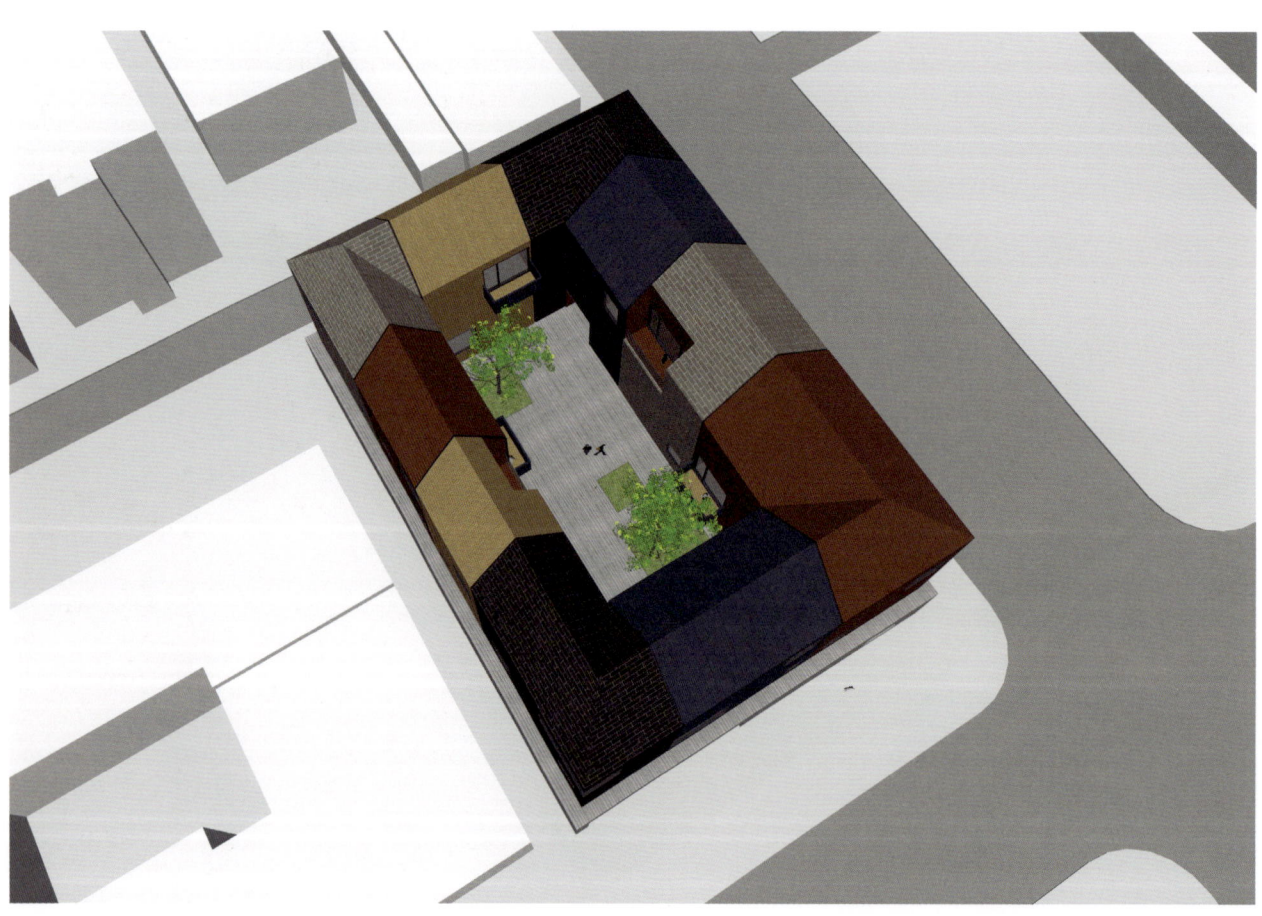

Los Angeles Communal Housing

The LA 1914 project is located in a mixed-use residential complex on a corner block allotment in Los Angeles, California, United States. Our primary focus for the design was to shape a project that would blend well with the character of the surrounding buildings, while maintaining a reasonable construction cost.

It is a three-story mixed-use building that includes a gallery, a café, and a bakery on the ground floor, with an uncovered courtyard. The café is intended for use as an outdoor terrace situated along the path, and in that sense it is connected to the courtyard to develop a sense of open space.

The building is managed by the client's son, and the requirements for the ground floor included a loading dock, a cozy rest area for employees, a computer room, a place to store equipment, and a private office space. In the case of the office, it is a small-scale space (staffed by three employees) that welcomes only a small number of visitors.

Los Angeles Communal Housing

Los Angeles Communal Housing

Los Angeles Communal Housing

The first floor was planned as a rental apartment, and the rooftop penthouse on the second floor would be used by the client's children. Through the courtyard connected to the units below, the space has been configured like small houses in a village clustered together. Considering the courtyard as a reference point, various alleyway-like terraces open toward the courtyard. The circulation makes the connection as one enters and exits the terraces and the courtyard.

Los Angeles Communal Housing

The partitioned masses according to the units appear to be open to the urban landscape, but a study of the elevation materials was necessary due to the nature of the private program. The mesh on the lower levels is a semi-permeable material that doesn't appear too closed off from the street, yet users remain freely connected from the inside.

The rental units on the first floor are aimed at facilitating smooth communication between neighbors. Units of seven different characters embrace a range of living styles.

PYEONGCHANG WINTER OLYMPICS STADIUM

Creating a new discursive field around the social responses for the recycling of temporary architecture and design for the Olympic Games

Pyeongchang, Gangwon Province, Korea | 2015

floating lightly on ground for to be dismantled after the event.

Pyeongchang Winter Olympics Stadium

Host to the 2018 Winter Olympics (officially known as the XXIII Olympic Winter Games), Pyeongchang is a pristine location surrounded by high mountain ranges in the middle of the Taebaek Mountains. Planned for temporary use over a brief period during the games, the 2018 Pyeongchang Winter Olympics Stadium was designed as a venue capable of hosting an international festival with minimal impact on nature and using the least amount of resources as possible while still linking both local residents and visitors from farther afield.

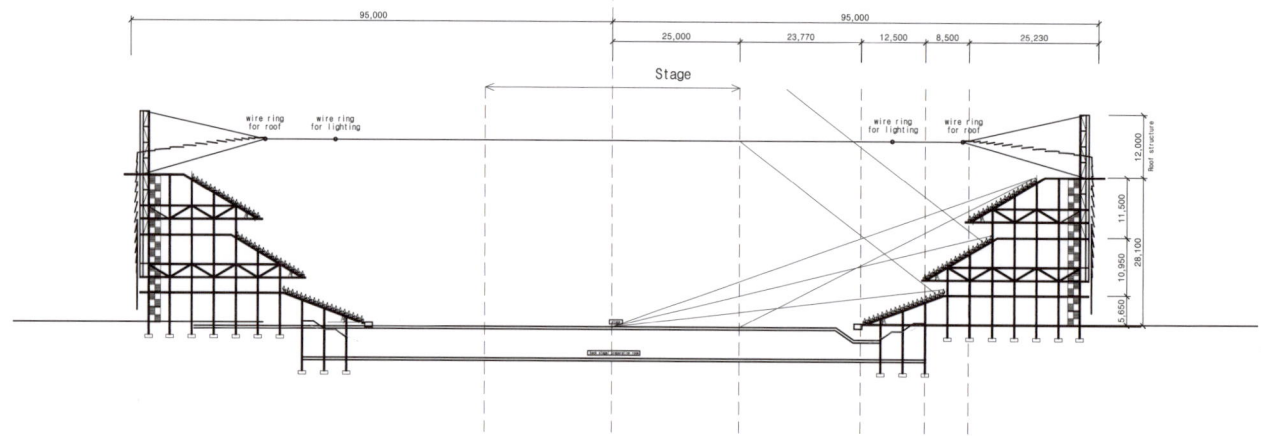

Section

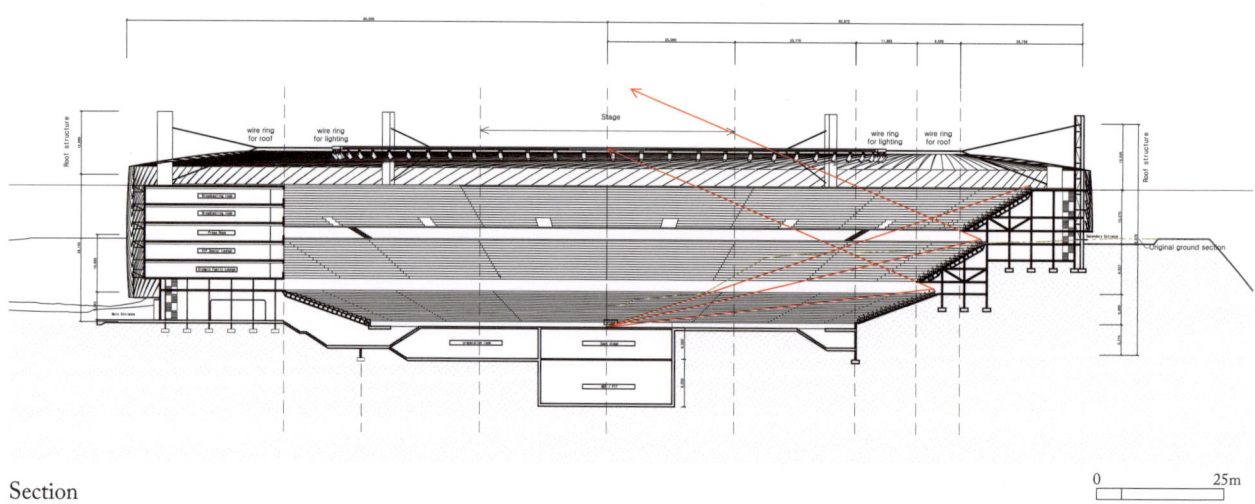

Section

Pyeongchang Winter Olympics Stadium

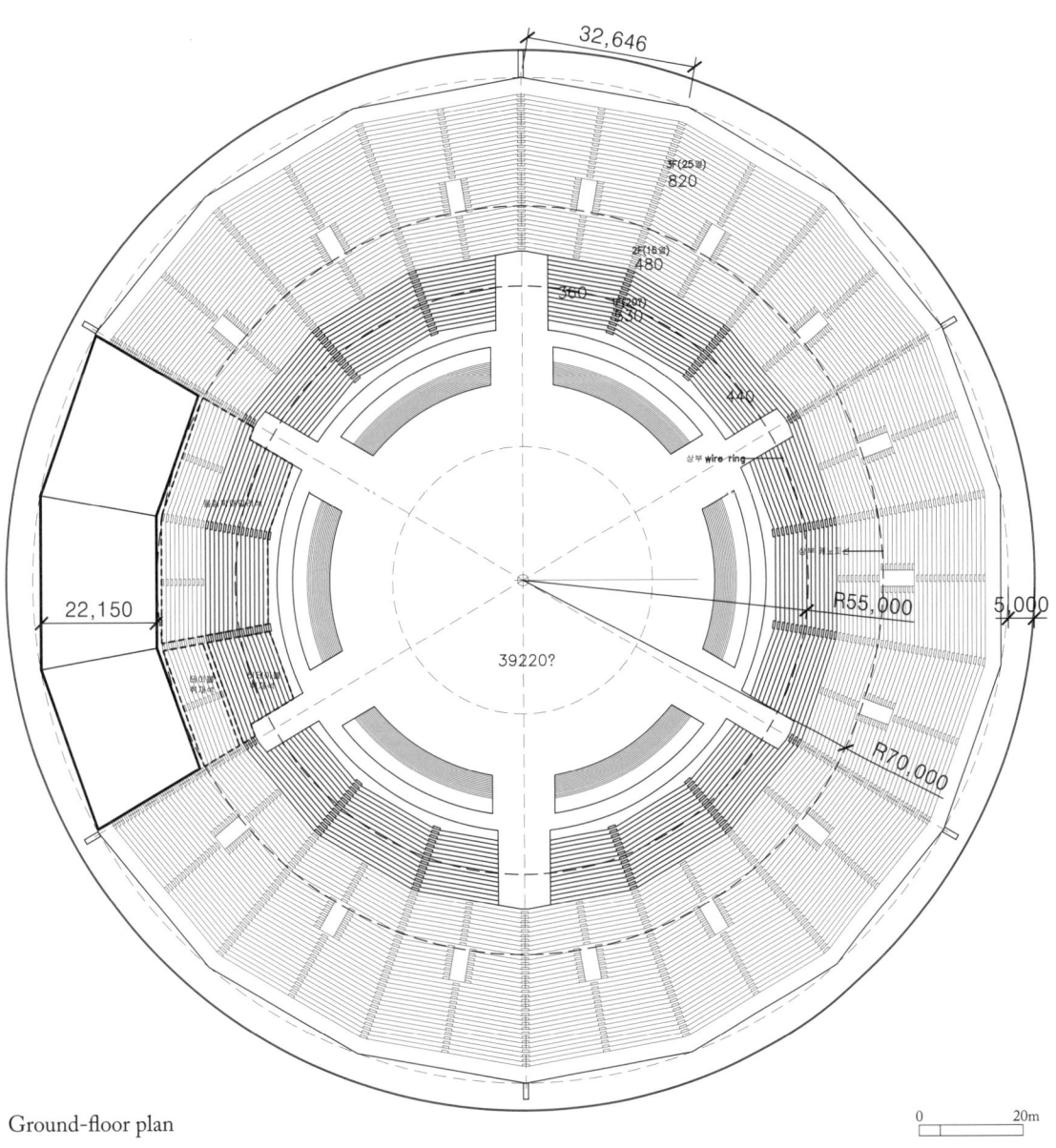

Ground-floor plan

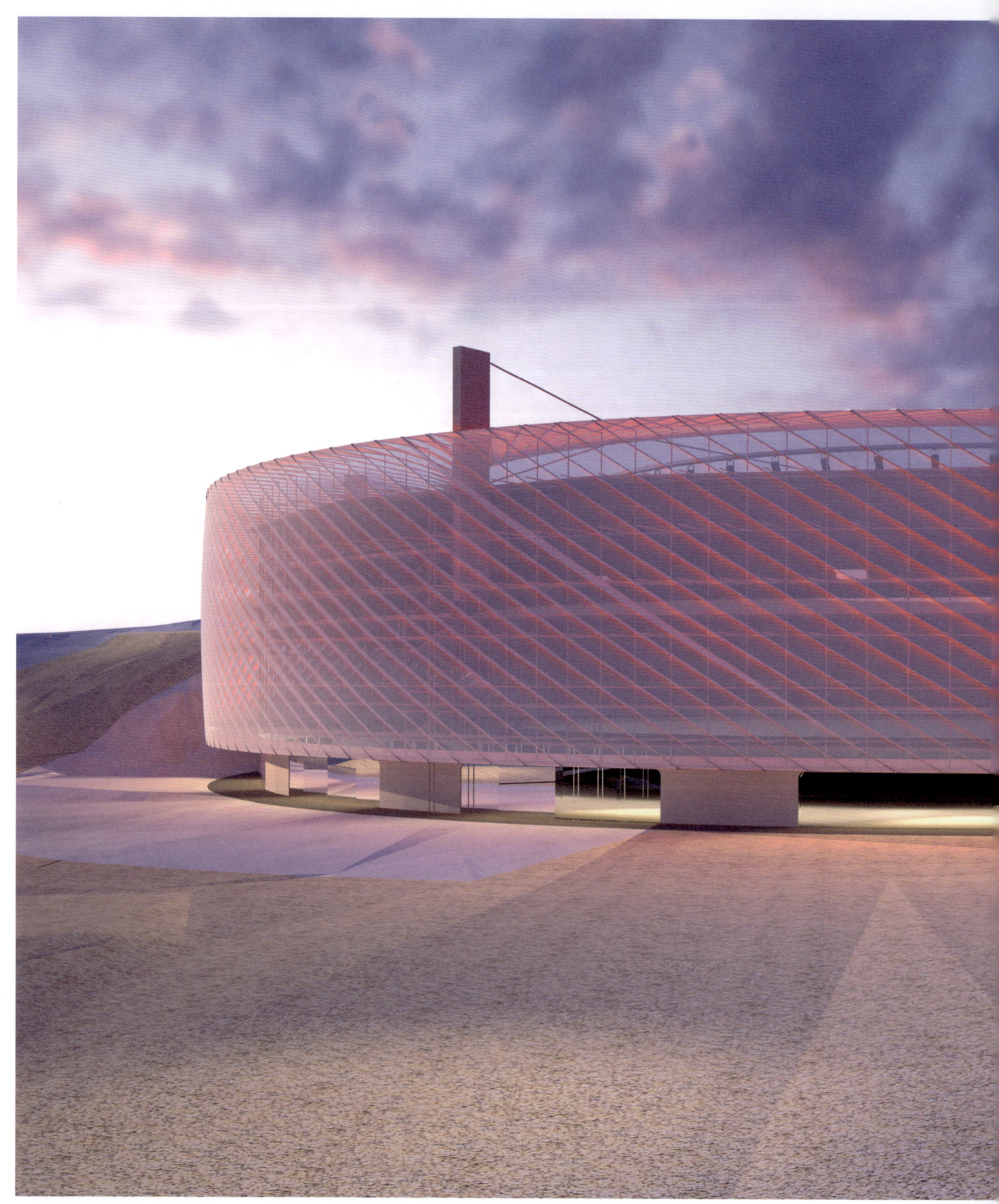

Pyeongchang Winter Olympics Stadium

Our concept did not place emphasis on a monumental building but sought the creation of a valuable narrative in the construction process. Our proposal for this new stadium took inspiration from the reinterpretation of the theme of the 2018 Winter Olympics, "Harmony and Convergence." Considering the unity to be achieved between nature, architecture, and people, we wanted to create a space that would make the smallest possible mark on nature by designing a small-scale building and forming a general consensus around its function and public channels of communication to make sure that the key function is understood. To this end, our concept focused on 98 percent use of recycling building components and to use only three materials where possible: steel and scaffolding, seating, and fabric.

The building is framed with steel and scaffolding, and its exterior is clad in fabric. In its concave circular form, the design aims to further extend accessibility to the games both acoustically and visually. Moreover, since the Olympic Winter Games are also held at night, the fabric used as the building's exterior subtly mutes the light emitted by the site, drawing it into a single soft light.

Pyeongchang Winter Olympics Stadium

Pyeongchang Winter Olympics Stadium

These international events do not end with the Olympics, but our hope is to place greater significance on the dismantling and recyclability of the buildings in the months post-event. Our proposition is for an international idea and design competition on the theme of using the structural components and materials of the dismantled building after the Olympics. This event-oriented building only exists during the ceremonies and is dismantled once the games are over. Its seating can be reused, but also the fabric and scaffolding both have enormous potential: whether they are to be used as tents, bedding, bags, or blankets for refugees. Through a proposed collaboration with the United Nations, our concept aims to promote physical and social responses to exchange and cycles of use in the future. We wish to highlight this: by the competition becoming an event that is more open and where different people such as students and designers participate, it aims to create a new discursive field around the Olympics.

Pyeongchang Winter Olympics Stadium

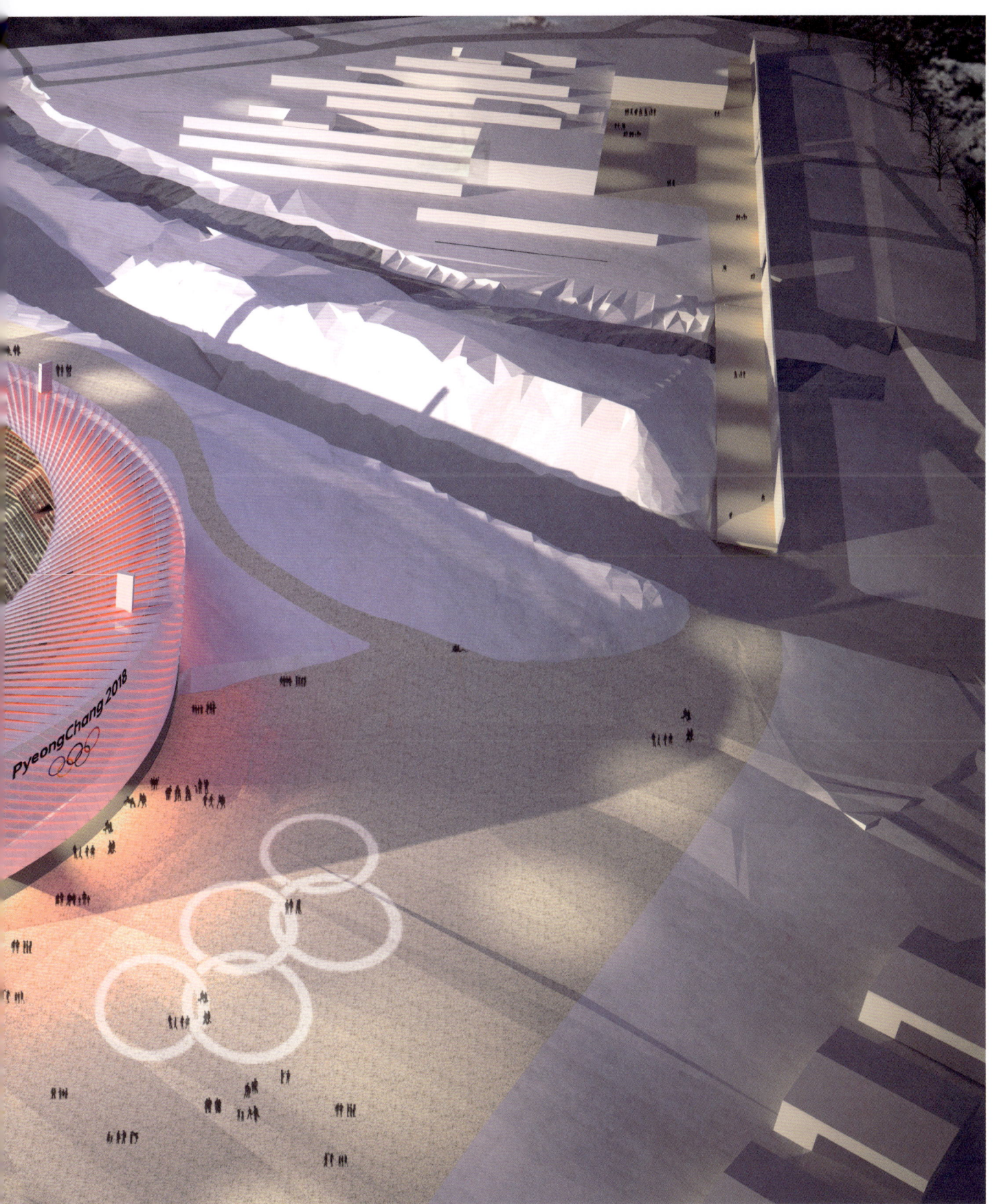

YOUNG HAK LEE SCULPTURE MUSEUM

A cultural place for contemplation of topography and nature, art, and design

Seorak Mountain, Gangwon Province, Korea | 2018

Young Hak Lee Sculpture Museum

Located in Pillye Village, Inje-gun, Gangwon Province, this museum project was designed to offer a space in which to view and experience the works of one of Korea's leading sculptors, Song Jeong Young Hak Lee (b. 1949). The artist's sculptural stone piece *Mulhwak* is a modern remake of the traditional work often seen in temples and in *hanok* (a traditional fourteenth-century-style Korean house) gardens. The artist's work here is remarkable in its elaborate sophistication and organicism when displayed inside. When it is placed at the center of the moss garden in his Suyu-dong house in Seoul, however, there its boundary disappears, revitalizing the work's pure, azure tone. This is the core idea behind the museum where Young Hak Lee's works would be exhibited.

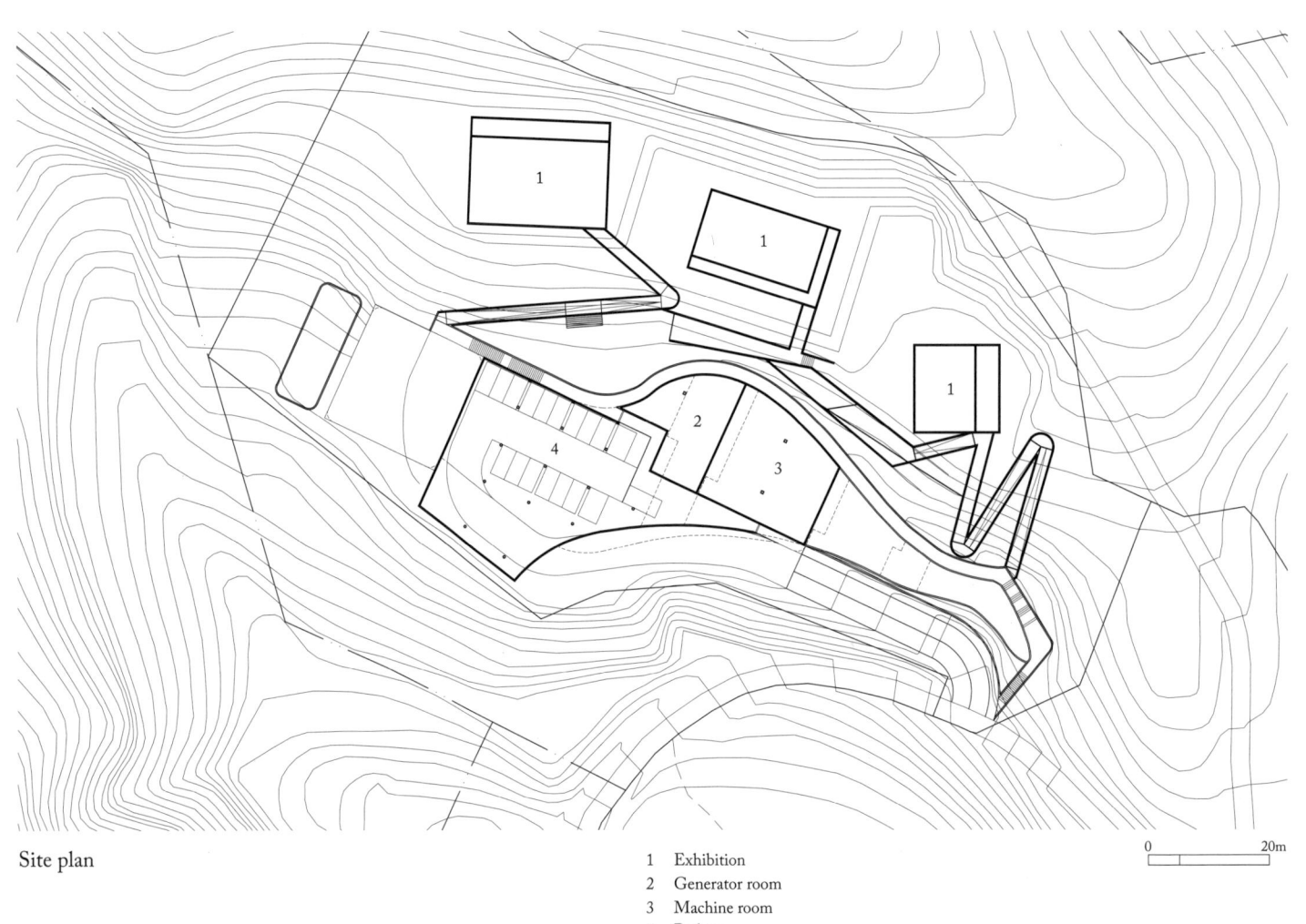

Site plan

1 Exhibition
2 Generator room
3 Machine room
4 Parking

Young Hak Lee Sculpture Museum

The Young Hak Lee Sculpture Museum is not just the simple creation of a cultural space, but of a space that nestles snugly into Seorak Mountain, where visitors can freely and casually walk around the sculptor's installations and the surrounding natural setting. The key point of the design is not just to appreciate art as an aesthetic object, but to contemplate it within its location in nature and to experience it within the dedicated space.

Young Hak Lee Sculpture Museum

Young Hak Lee Sculpture Museum

Young Hak Lee Sculpture Museum

The key concepts of the proposal were to position the museum according to its shape and flow, drawing on the existing sloped terrace-shaped topography, and to design it with minimal impact to the mountainscape's natural setting. The surrounding landscape is channelled so as to create a birch forest, and simple walls are erected to create a more harmonious form. A water garden is naturally situated within the topography in front of the museum, and the entrance path is designed to flow along with the garden. Planned as an annex, the exhibition hall is situated as if it were embedded in the terrain, configured as a space that contrasts darkness with light.

PILLYE VILLAGE, SEORAK MOUNTAIN

A therapeutic villa to provide for those seeking healing of the mind and body

Seorak Mountain, Gangwon Province, Korea | 2018

Pillye Village, Seorak Mountain

This project is for the construction of a villa located in Pillye Village, Inje-gun, Gangwon Province, deep within the natural beauty of Seorak Mountain. The concept behind the complex was to create a therapeutic place of healing, and the villa places an emphasis on providing comfortable lodgings for visitors who seek restorative practices for body and mind. We devised a space and layout that celebrates the wide-open spaces of the natural environment while also allowing visitors to enjoy the natural landscape from within their own lodgings, protecting individual privacy, and encouraging individual communion with nature.

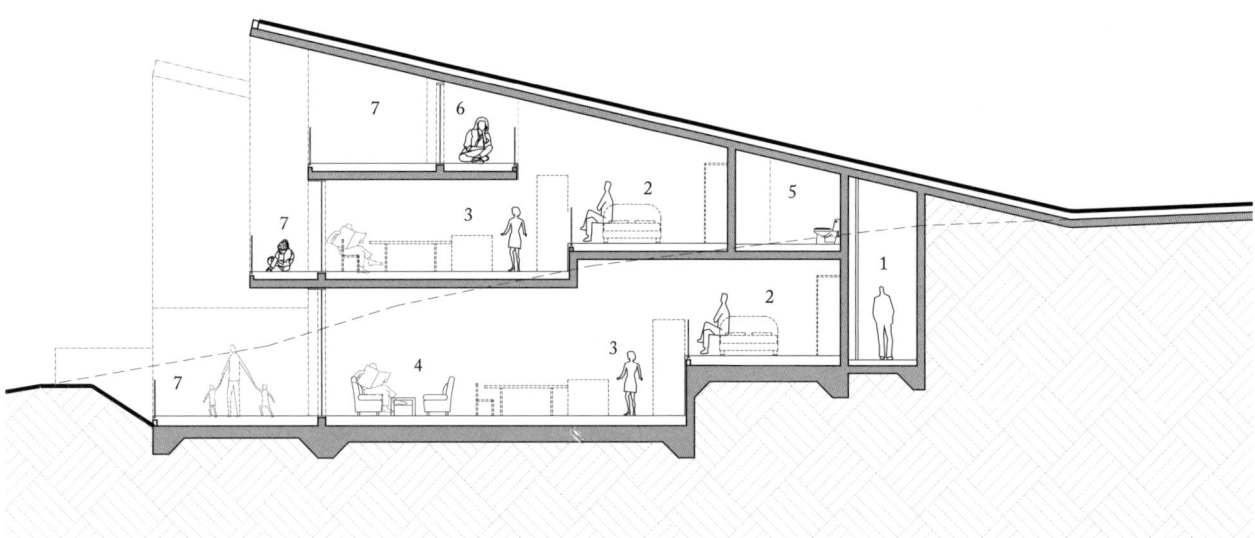

Section

1 Corridor
2 Bedroom
3 Kitchen
4 Living room
5 Restroom
6 Tea room
7 Exterior deck

Pillye Village, Seorak Mountain

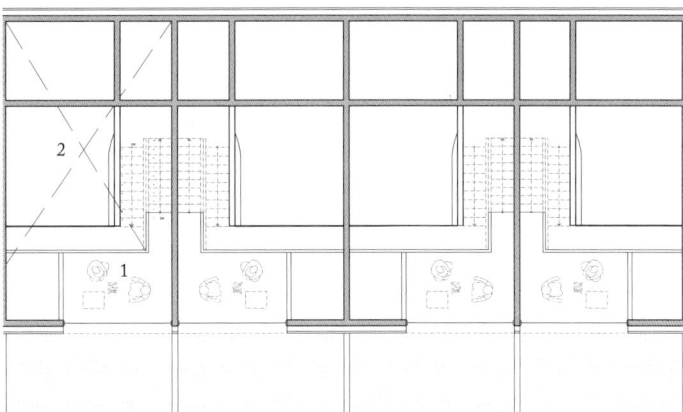

Second-floor plan

1 Tea room
2 Open to below

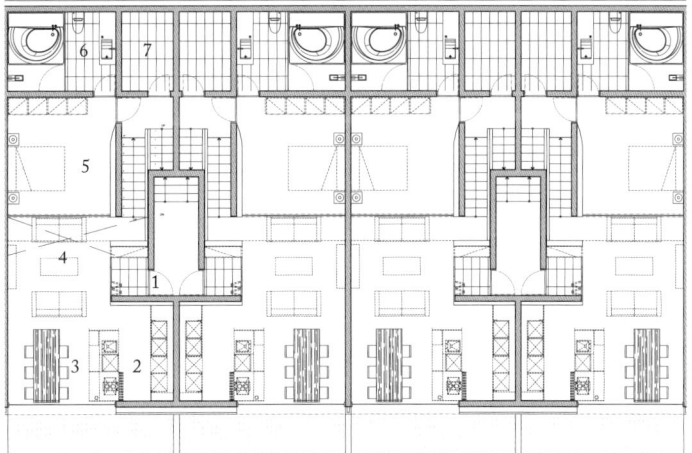

First-floor plan

1 Unit 2 entrance
2 Kitchen
3 Dining
4 Lounge
5 Bedroom
6 Restroom
7 Utility room

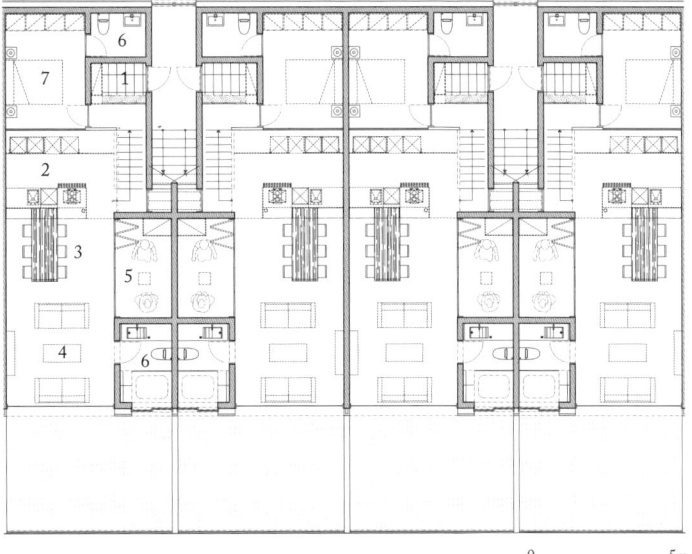

Ground-floor plan

1 Unit 1 entrance
2 Kitchen
3 Dining
4 Lounge
5 Tea room
6 Restroom
7 Bedroom

The villa was designed to organically integrate within the existing topography, its shape representing a stone lying on the ground along the slope of the mountain. It was positioned by drawing upon the lines and planes of the surrounding mountains, and its mass was divided into parts so that a view of the range opens up through the gap. The ground conditions of the site were that of downward sloping terrain, but the roof of the villa is tilted up, forming a natural and balanced line of perspective. When viewed from above it was designed to look completely unbarred, positioned in a formative manner by ensuring light from the interior could escape through the spaces in between. The roof is deliberately covered by the landscape so that, when viewed from the back, the building would become one with nature.

Pillye Village, Seorak Mountain

Pillye Village, Seorak Mountain

Pillye Village, Seorak Mountain

The site features a steep drop, like a cliff, with mountains spreading out at the front. The four-story building is illuminated to the south, opening up a view toward the landscape. To establish a more rational structure, construction did not involve any changes to the existing terrain's level, which minimized the amount of soil to be excavated and enhanced the overall efficiency and timescale of the project. The shear-wall-structured floor plans, which are long in both the front and back, have also been designed according to an open plan and stacked vertically so that visitors can survey the encircling scenery from anywhere within the interior.

AYU25 BOTANICAL CAFÉ

Creating architecture deeply related to the
philosophy of the AYU25 brand

Namyangju, Gyeonggi Province, Korea | 2020

roof plate, vertical walls,
supporting / bent
squeezing into the spaces!

dwg
not below

AYU25 Botanical Café

The proposal for a café and herb garden for the cosmetic brand AYU25 is deeply related to the beliefs and philosophy of the brand itself. The brand seeks to promote human wellness and healing through the wholesome experience of nature. This includes not only the use of botanical ingredients but also the stimulation of our senses through aromatherapy. It is the brand's conviction that nature, and our experience of nature, is the key element that refocuses our state of mind and body to its fullness. Following this belief, the architecture of this project was planned to maximize the conditions already present in the surrounding nature.

AYU25 Botanical Café

The proposed flat, rectangular plot of land faces a wondrous expanse of nature: the Bukhan River stretches right across the width of the site, and the charismatic mountain range, including Bukhan Mountain, are in full view. The proposed building was deliberately rotated to face the most dramatic view of the mountain. The shape of the building is neither a complete circle nor a perfect geometry but rather a slightly deformed circular shape that serves to neutralize the somewhat artificial and sharp edges of the plot boundary. Once inside the building, the view of the mountain and river is spread along the panoramic windows. The herb garden that is gently encircled by the building leads visitors outside and continuously along the stepped platform of the roof. The entire experience of the project is a choreographed sequence that maximizes the visitor's experience of the site.

AYU25 Botanical Café

AYU25 Botanical Café

AYU25 Botanical Café

NEUTRA HOUSE— STUDIO ADDITION

A dramatic consolidation with nature and cultivation of a theatrical effect for a midcentury modern residence

Missoula, Montana, United States | 2014

Neutra House—Studio Addition

This is an extension project for the Mosby House originally designed by Richard Neutra, who was made famous by works such as the Case Study Houses of the late 1940s and was one of the foremost practitioners of midcentury modern residences in the United States. Located in Montana, the site is positioned on a hill overlooking the Dean Stone Mountain and University Mountain at a distance. Situated in a residential district on the outskirts of the downtown district, Mosby House has views out across the cityscape to the west and over a more natural landscape to the east. The location and height of the windows in the existing Neutra House were designed according to the placement of the furniture and the lifestyle of its users, and so the interior was designed to favor one's ability to surveil the surrounding environment.

The clients, who are a married couple (she a fashion designer, and he a professor of the Film Department at the local university), are both fond of dramatic and creative spaces. They requested an extension to the garage studio to include a studio and parking space. In order to design a space most suited and sensitive to the merits of this site and its unique conditions, and so as to cultivate a more theatrical spatial effect, the new building was designed to become a new, separate mass rather than as a connected element of the existing house.

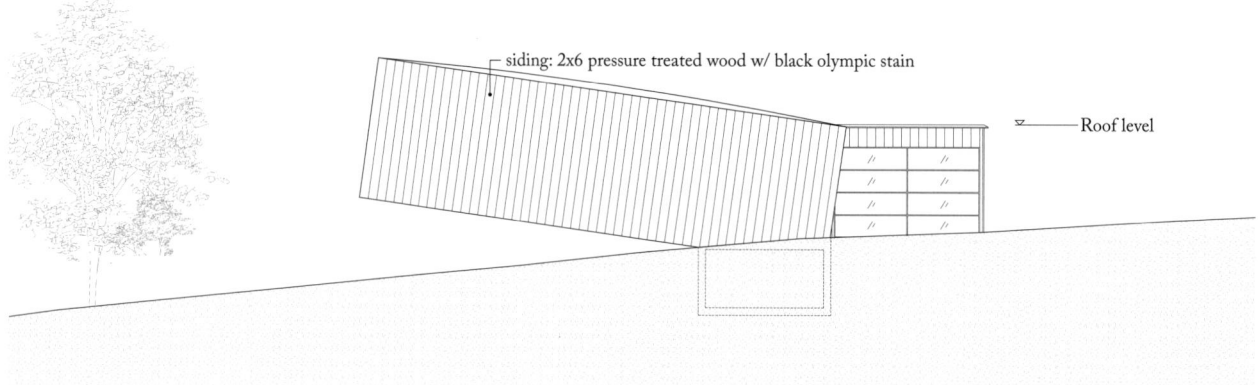

South elevation

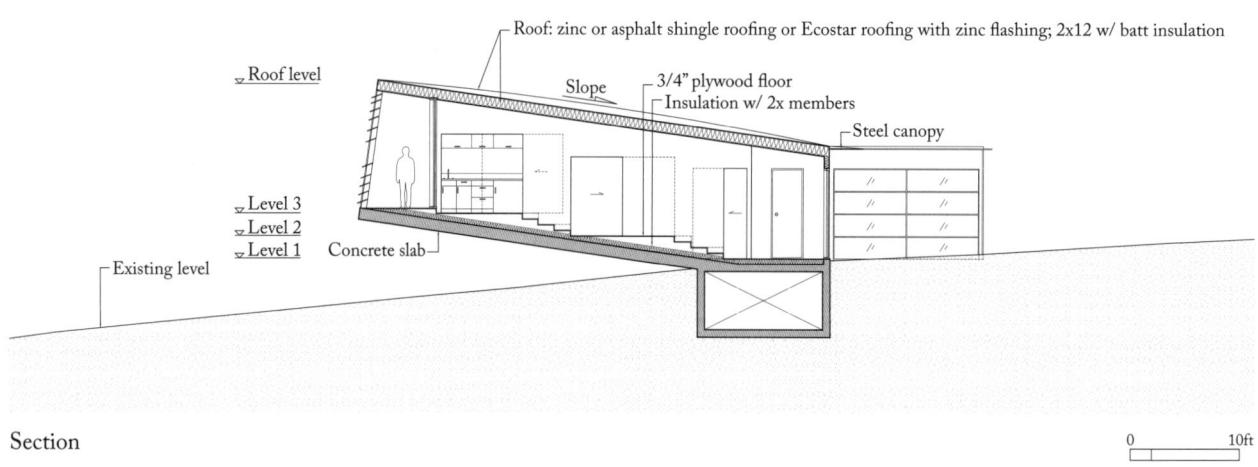

Section

Neutra House—Studio Addition

Site plan

Neutra House—Studio Addition

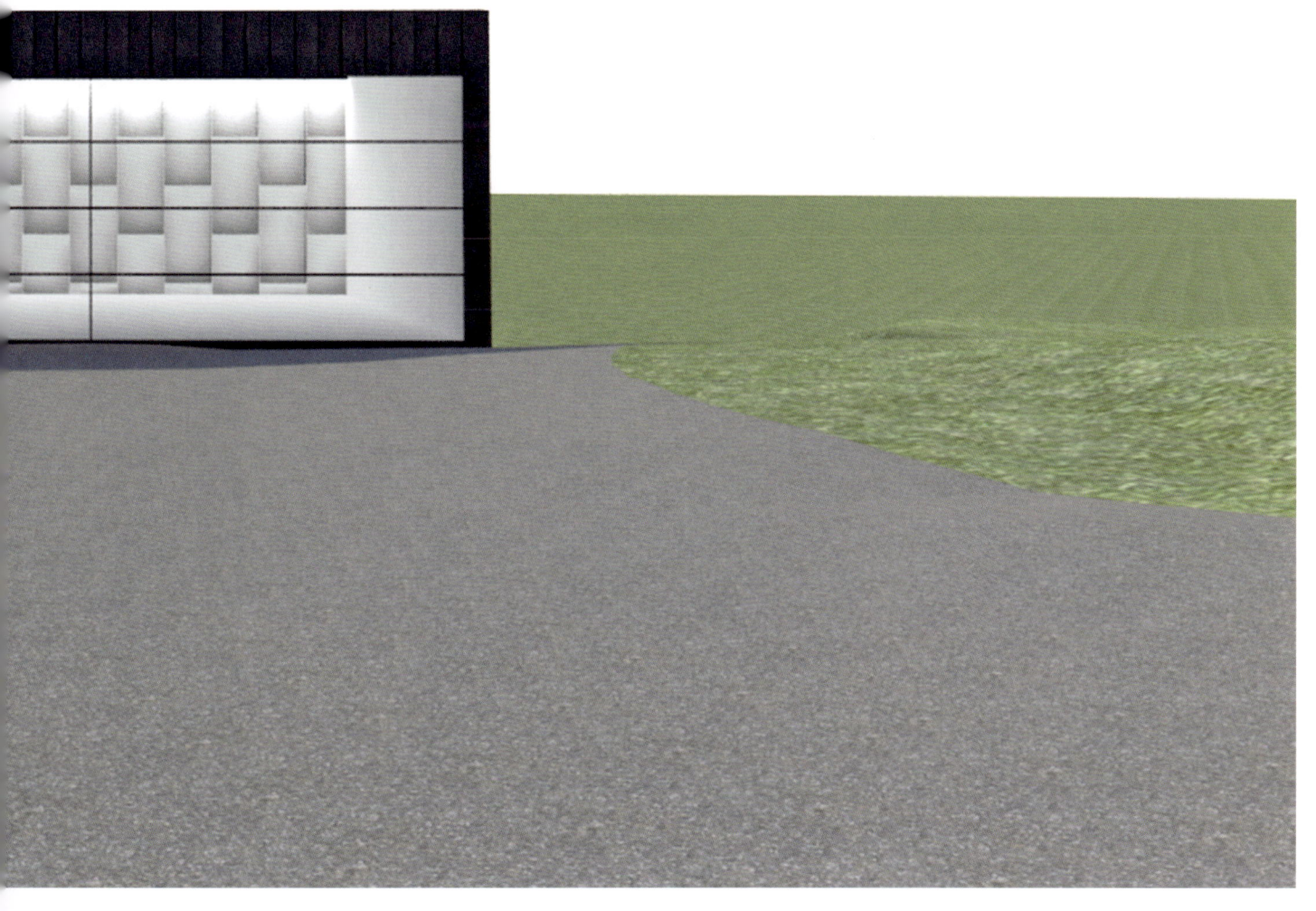

Designed to sit upon the topography of the mound next to the existing Mosby House, this garage studio was positioned in a way so as to be seen directly when one enters the site, close to the existing house, eliminating any downside to circulation. The plan was also designed to follow the flow of the topography, by which the bedroom and studio parking lot were positioned on different levels to create a space that would stretch out as if one climbs a hill. This was guided by a concept of consolidation with nature, to become a structure as if rising from the hill on which the building is located.

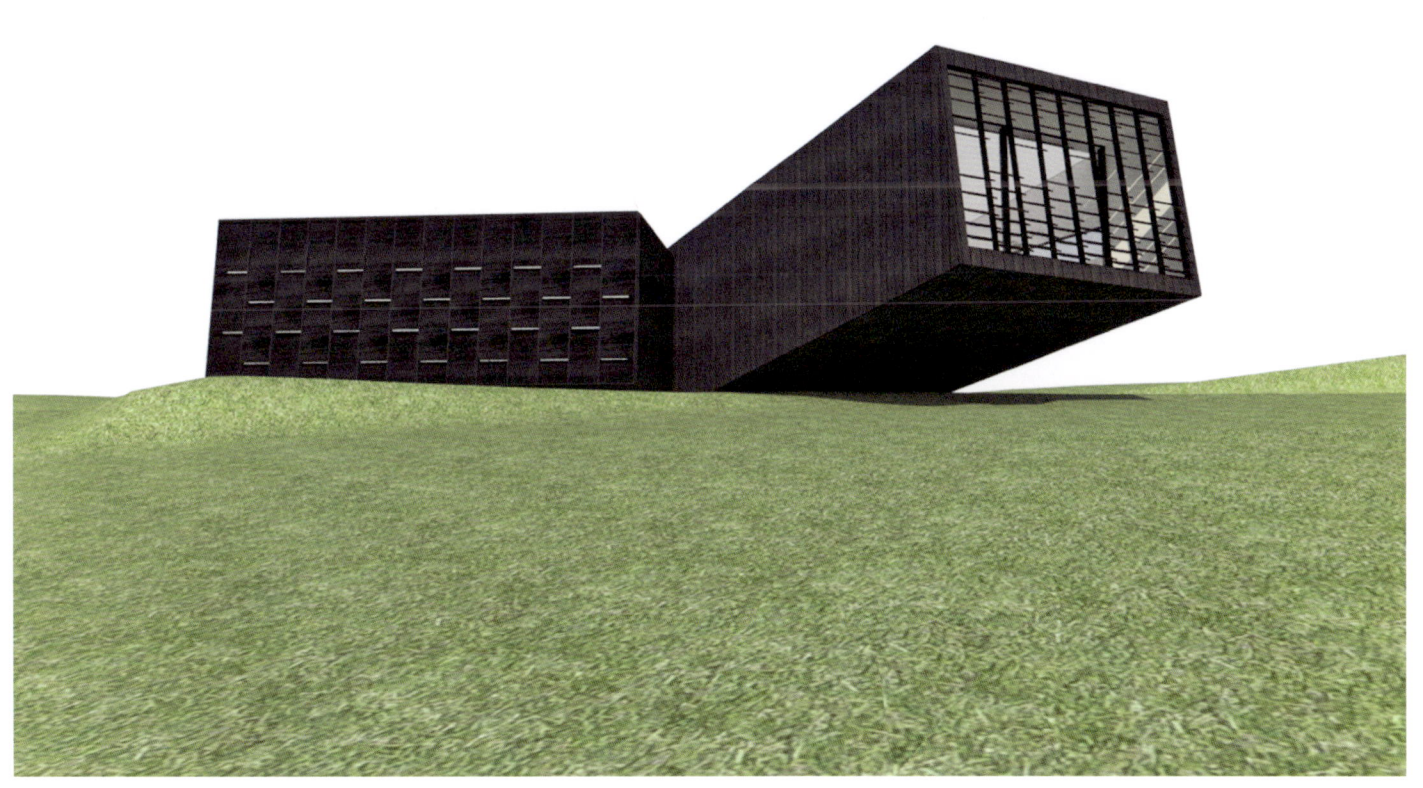

Neutra House—Studio Addition

Moreover, a floor-to-ceiling window was conceived by floating the mass in order to obtain a view of Dean Stone Mountain and University Mountain in the distance. This is in conjunction with the interior design of Neutra House, which prioritizes the surrounding landscape, thus one can experience stunning Montana sunsets from the studio's floor-to-ceiling window. By using plywood to design screens and applying them to the mass, the lighting can be adjusted with assured privacy. The plywood screen was designed by reinterpreting the sidings often used in American houses.

AHN CHOONG-KUN MEMORIAL LIBRARY

Taking shape not only within the formal dimensions of architecture, but also through its metaphysical dimensions

Paju, Gyeonggi Province, Korea | 2017

Ahn Choong-kun Memorial Library

The project intended to create a memorial space to commemorate the life of Ahn Choong-kun (1879–1910), a Korean independence activist and pan-Asianist. The project would take shape not only within in the formal dimensions of architecture also in more profound ways through its metaphysical dimensions.

In terms of its typology, the library is an example of "pathway" architecture. While the main programmatic volume of the library is nestled deep within the heart of a forest, a large part of the site is occupied by a winding external circulation path that leads to the main library. Visitors are invited to walk along these serene forest walkways, listen out for bird song, and breathe in the scent of floral blossoms. Beams of warm sunlight and the dance of a gentle breeze felt along this path compel each visitor to contemplate Ahn Choong-kun's spiritual worldview. The memorial library building, rather than emphasizing its physicality, is a spatial device that brings about a process of communication and unification with nature and resonates with memories of Ahn Choong-kun.

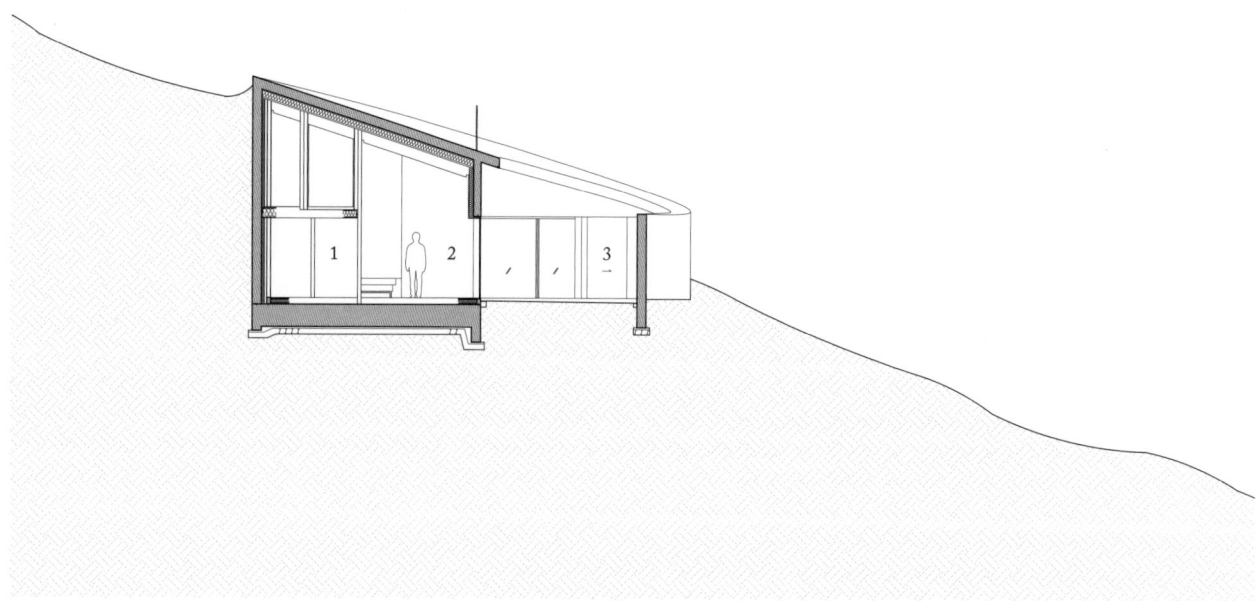

Section

1 Exhibition
2 Courtyard
3 Library

Ahn Choong-kun Memorial Library

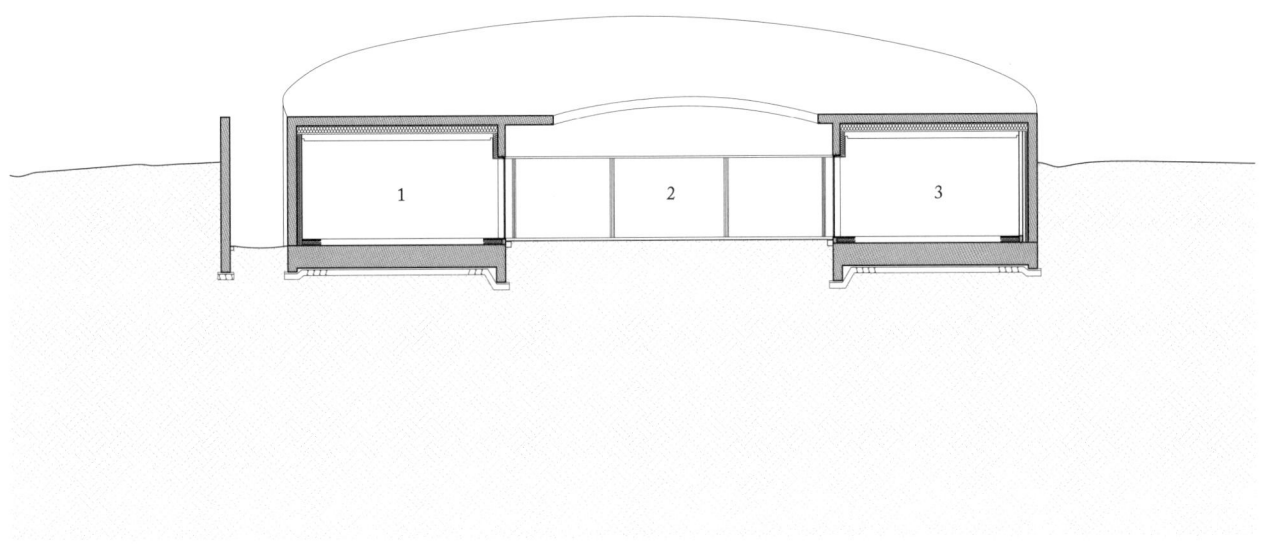

Section

1 Exhibition
2 Courtyard
3 Library

Ahn Choong-kun Memorial Library

416 MEMORIAL PARK AND MUSEUM

The souls of the victims, symbolized by various light sources, all converge into one light

Ansan, Gyeonggi Province, Korea | 2021

땅으로부터 출발해 하늘을향해 떴다,
안정과 희망의 메세지...

416 Memorial Park and Museum

We devised a proposal for a memorial park to commemorate the victims of the 2014 Sewol ferry disaster. The memorial park will be located in the city of Ansan where many of the 304 victims—pupils on an excursion—were from, and will be a space for mourning and a remembrance. It will also act as an educational space, prompting ongoing discussions on life and safety, and the responsibility of the state.

On the edge of Hwarang Reservoir, the new 416 Memorial Park was planned to commemorate the Sewol ferry disaster victims and share the pain of their families. Our plan begins with a message of sublimation, starting with the deep echo of the earth, and leading to a sense of safety and hope toward the sky.

The aim was to avoid an urban sense of scale. The site should simply be an undefined open space available to anyone. Imposing an urban scale structure or forceful connections to it would damage the inherent nature of the land. The park should subtly merge itself with its surroundings through the flow of land and the forest.

416 Memorial Park and Museum

416 Memorial Park and Museum

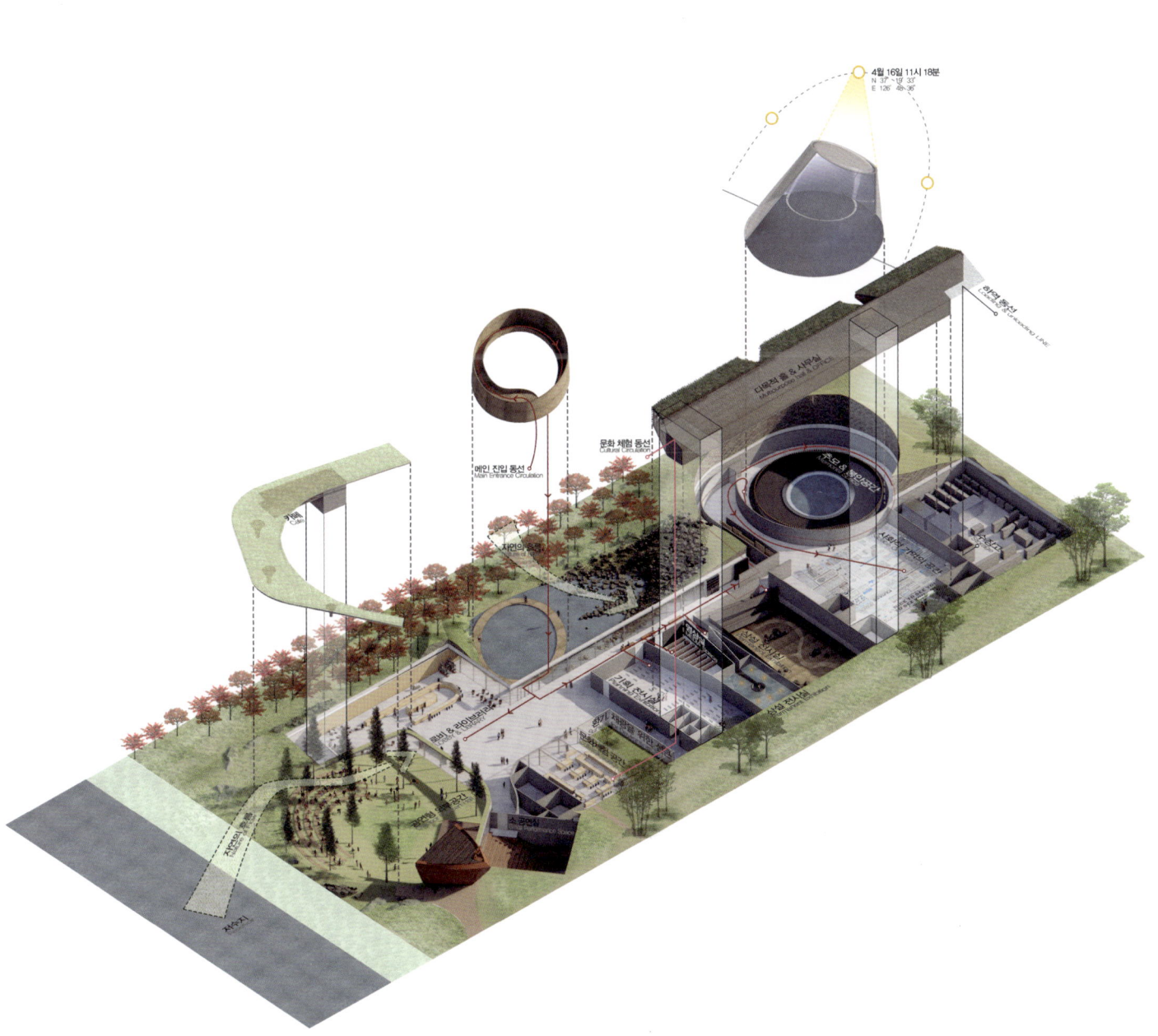

416 Memorial Park and Museum

416 Memorial Park and Museum

416 Memorial Park and Museum

The 304 crepe myrtle trees planted in the park represent each of the victims. Each tree will have a bench next to it to provide a place of comfort for the victims' families and a shelter that transcends time. The piles of stones piled up on the hills seen from the entry ramp symbolizes desperate memories and reminds visitors of the pain experienced by each bereaved family.

For the museum, on the anniversary of the disaster at exactly 11:18 a.m. on April 16, dazzling interplay between light and shadow over the sky in the enshrinement room sublimates the memory of that tragic day. The souls of the victims, symbolized by various light sources, all converge into one light in the enshrinement room. The light leads one from the enshrinement room to the vast green field that is the space of resurrection and vitality.

This commemorative place, open from the ground toward the sky, contains a message of safety and hope.

416 Memorial Park and Museum

Commemoration and enshrinment space

8:00

9:00

10:00

11:18 (4/16)

14:00

16:00

HONGCHEON HOTEL

Creating an immersive, solitary retreat within nature

Hongcheon, Gangwon Province, Korea | 2013

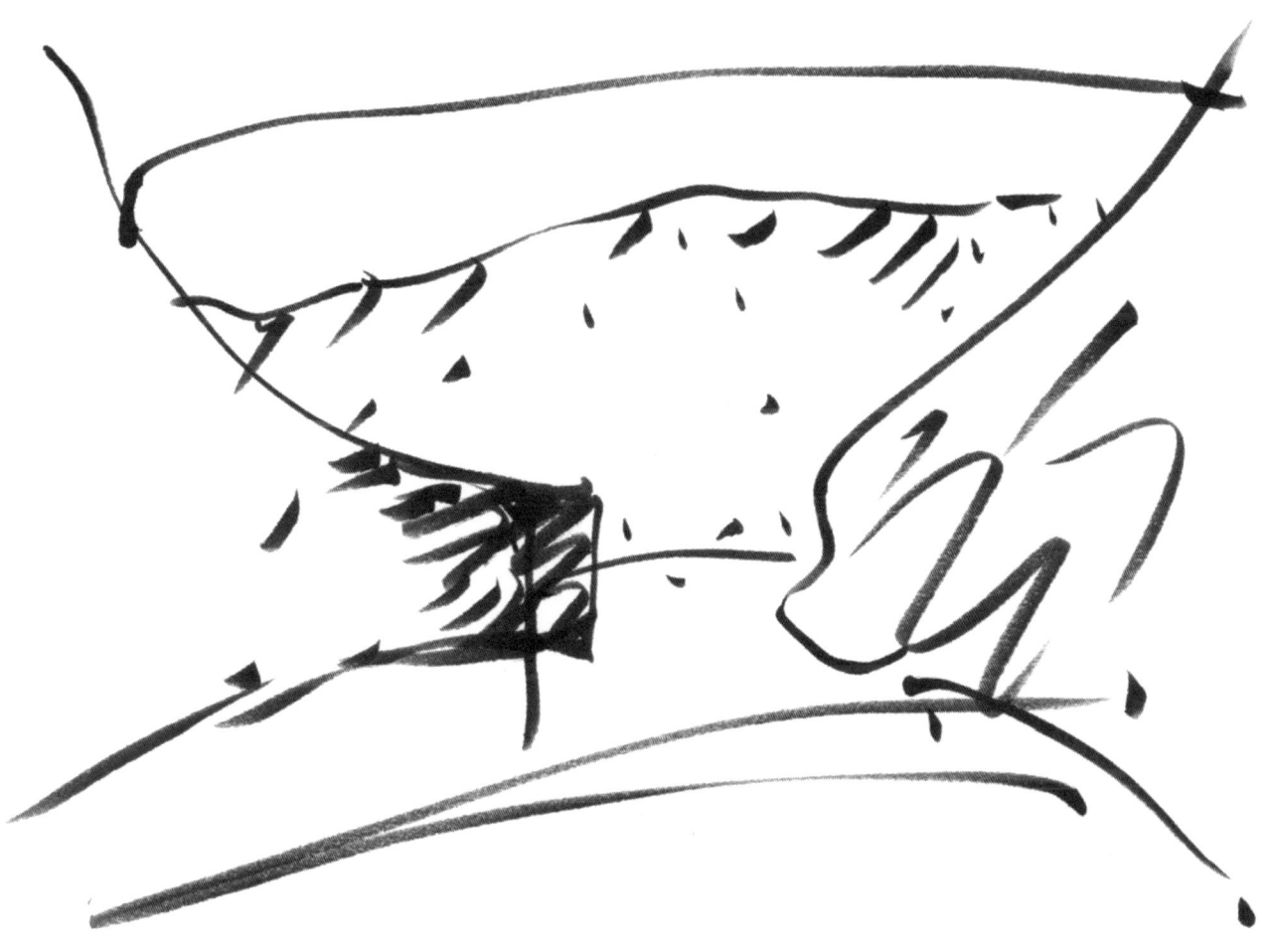

Site plan

Hongcheon Hotel

This residential project takes its primary focus from two characteristic features of the site: the uninterrupted panoramic views of Hongcheon River, and the geometric complexity of the site boundaries. The winding form of the villa takes its shape from the idiosyncratic geometry of the site and we used this visual language to introduce private alleys and entryways that lead to each villa unit. We wanted the sequential experience offered by these secretive alleyways to be reminiscent of an immersive, restful, and solitary retreat within nature. Meanwhile, the landscape-like structure blends into the existing topography and allows the building to be read as an extension of this surrounding natural realm.

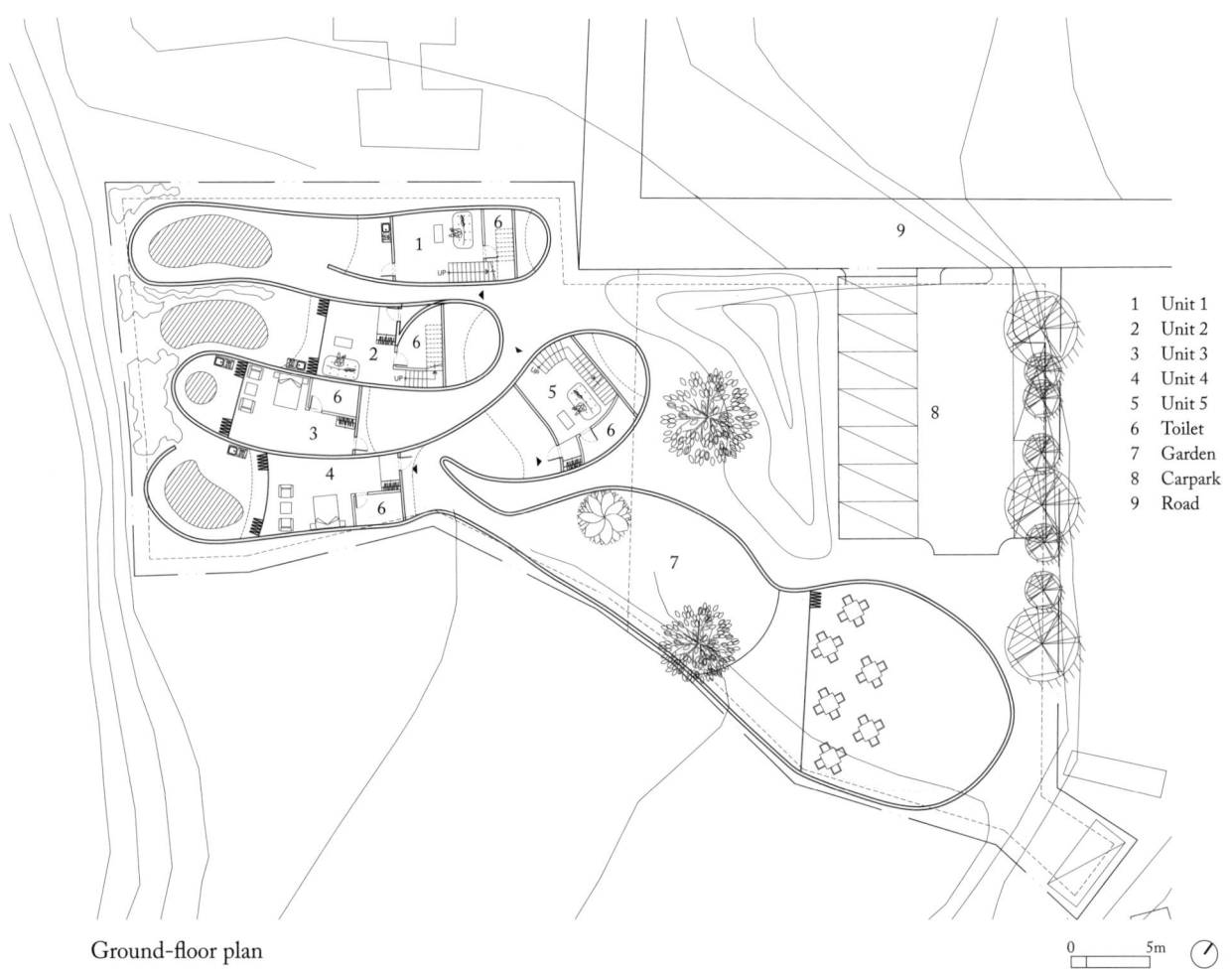

Ground-floor plan

1 Unit 1
2 Unit 2
3 Unit 3
4 Unit 4
5 Unit 5
6 Toilet
7 Garden
8 Carpark
9 Road

Hongcheon Hotel

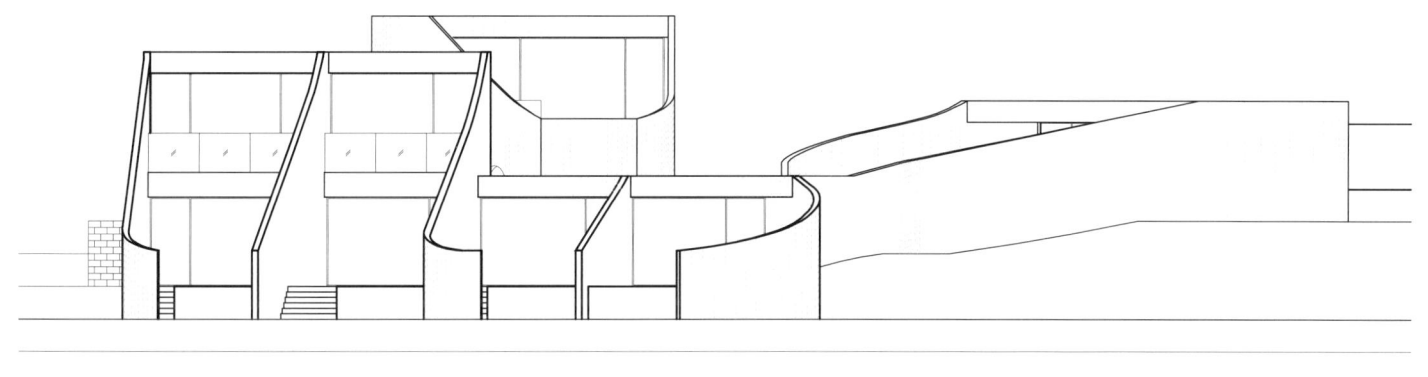

West elevation

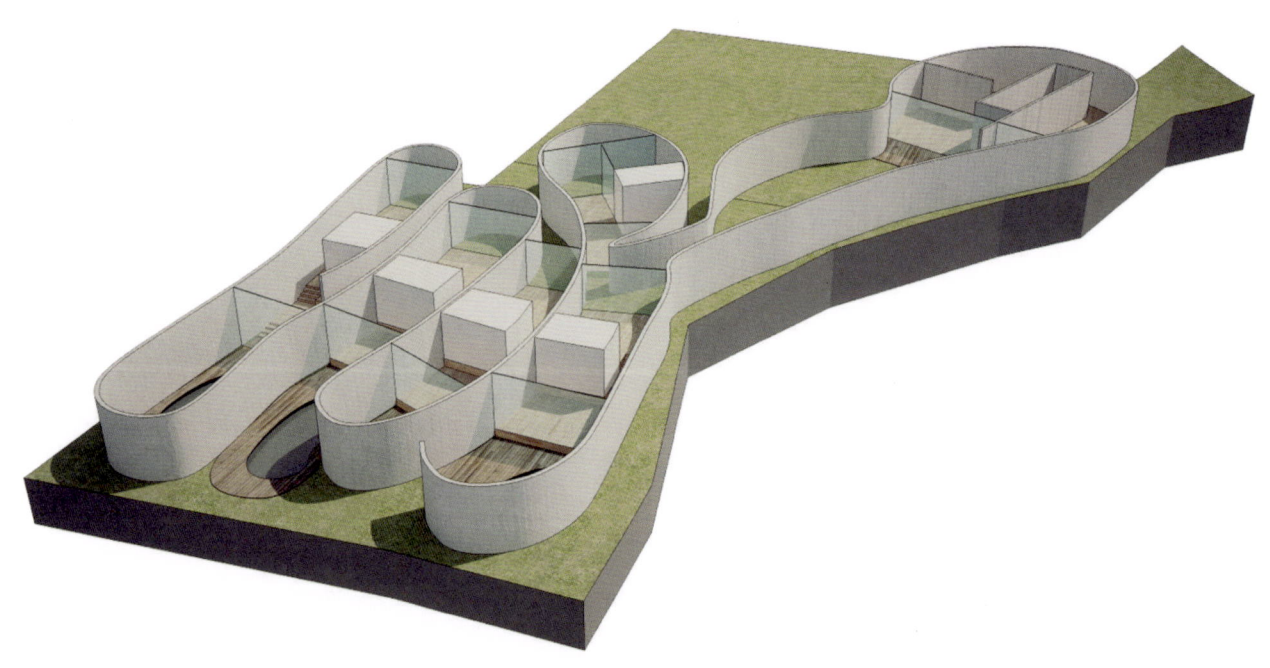

Hongcheon Hotel

BANGDONG-RI PREFAB HOUSE

Following the continuous language of the surrounding mountains while maintaining privacy

Inje-gun, Gangwon Province, Korea | 2017

thin PC panels & the gaps between

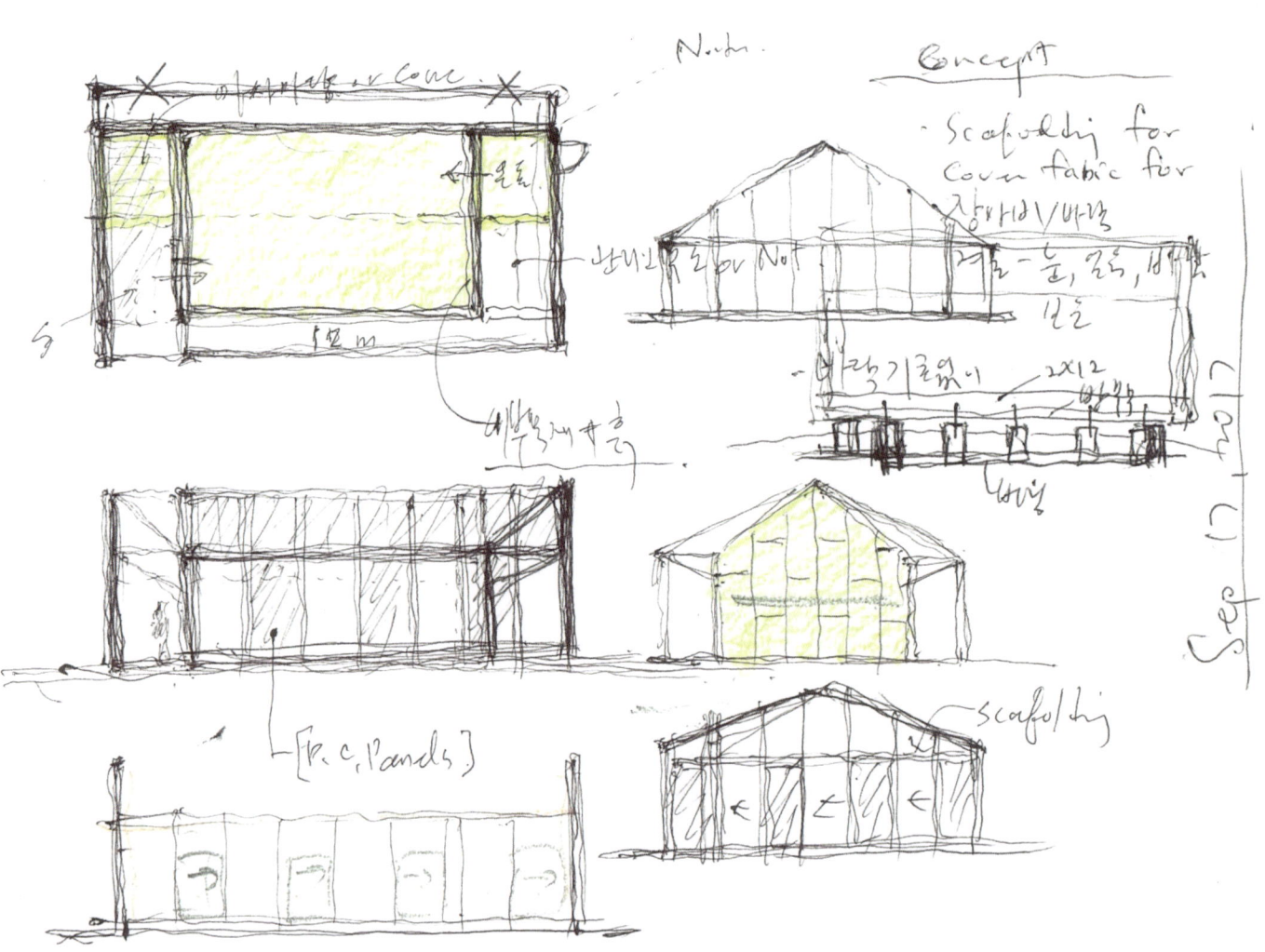

Bangdong-ri Prefab House

This is a housing project located in Inje-gun, Gangwon Province. Set against the backdrop of Seorak Mountain, a spot that attracts many hikers with its rich and abundant landscape, the site of this project is in a favorable location with the mountain at the back and facing a flowing expanse of water. However, the site's location deep in the mountain resulted in poor construction conditions and no electricity supply, so there was also a need for alternative energy sources.

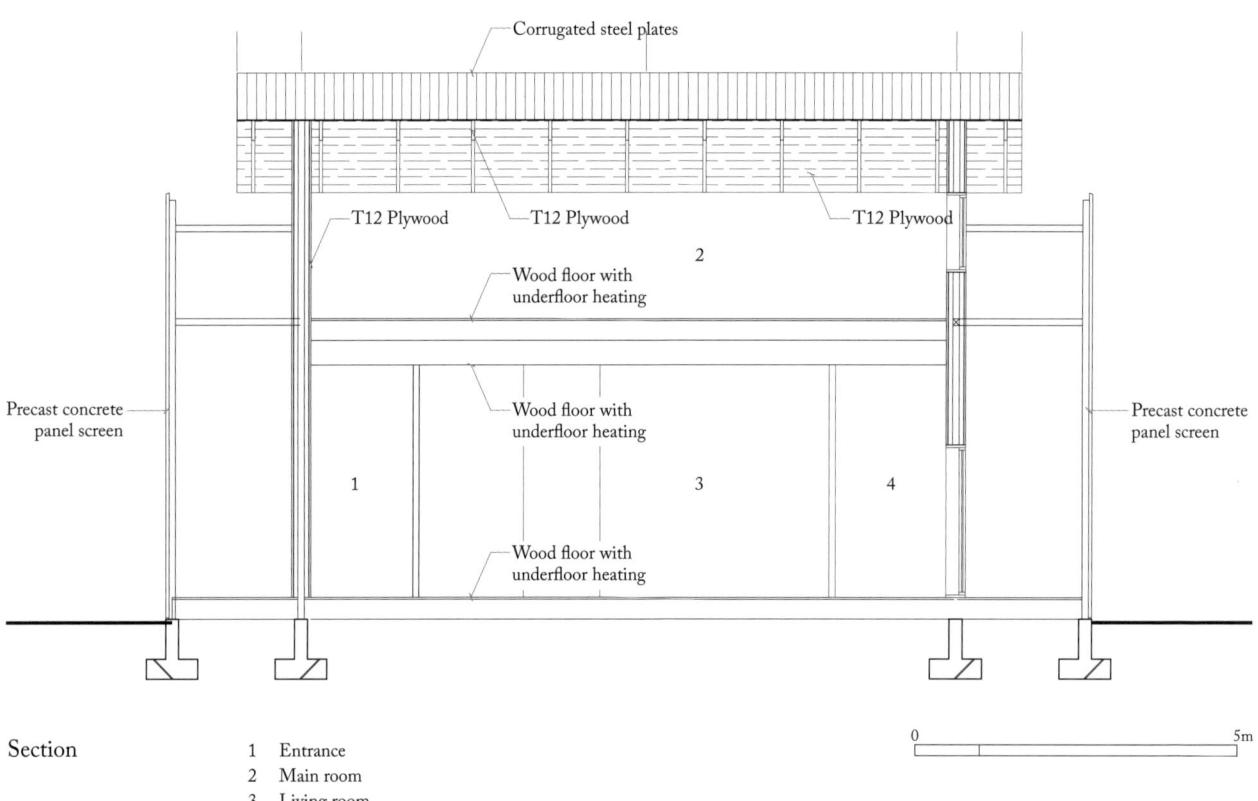

Section
1 Entrance
2 Main room
3 Living room
4 Kitchen

Bangdong-ri Prefab House

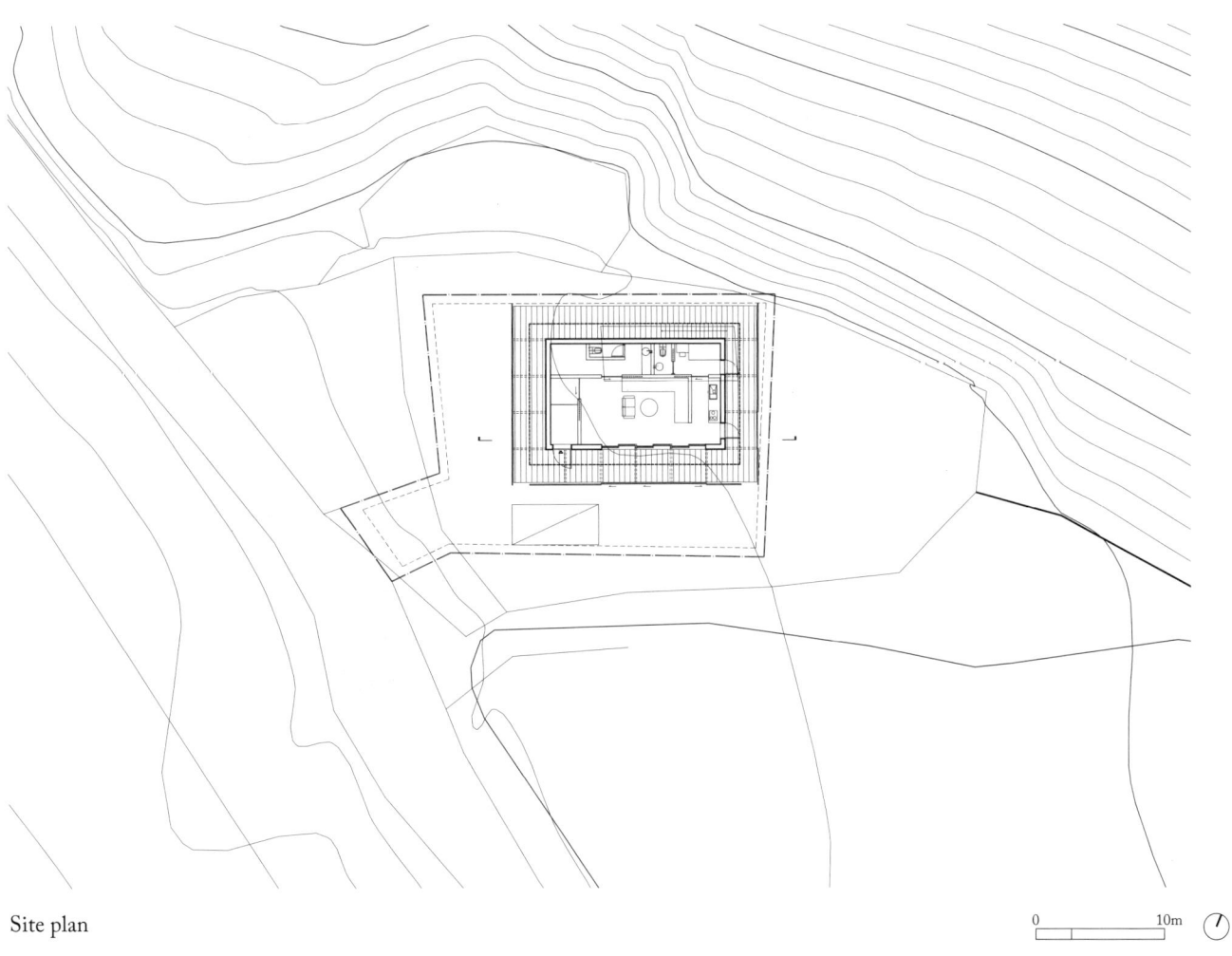

Site plan

The client enjoys hiking and wanted to use it as his occasional weekend house for a family of four. He hoped for it to be self-sufficent housing with simple functions such as a living room, kitchen, guest room, and bathroom. The client wanted it to be designed to resemble a simple and comfortable warehouse, rather than a luxurious house. Also, as the site was to be located on a roadside used by many hikers, it was also important to block views from passersby.

Bangdong-ri Prefab House

Bangdong-ri Prefab House

In order to resolve the problem of accessibility to the site, we decided to use a structure that would be easy to assemble, and to use precast concrete panels on the exterior façade facilitating easy transportation and assembly. In this way, a double façade could be constructed to form layers, adjust ventilation and lighting, and create a sense of a cozy indoor space even though it was outside. Some of the precast concrete was shaped into sliding doors, creating a simple form that provides views of the surrounding greenery when open and obscures views from the exterior when closed.

Bangdong-ri Prefab House

FOUR PIECE HOUSING

Creating a new discursive field around the social responses for the recycle of temporary architecture and design and the Olympic Games

Mangmi-dong, Busan, Korea | 2017

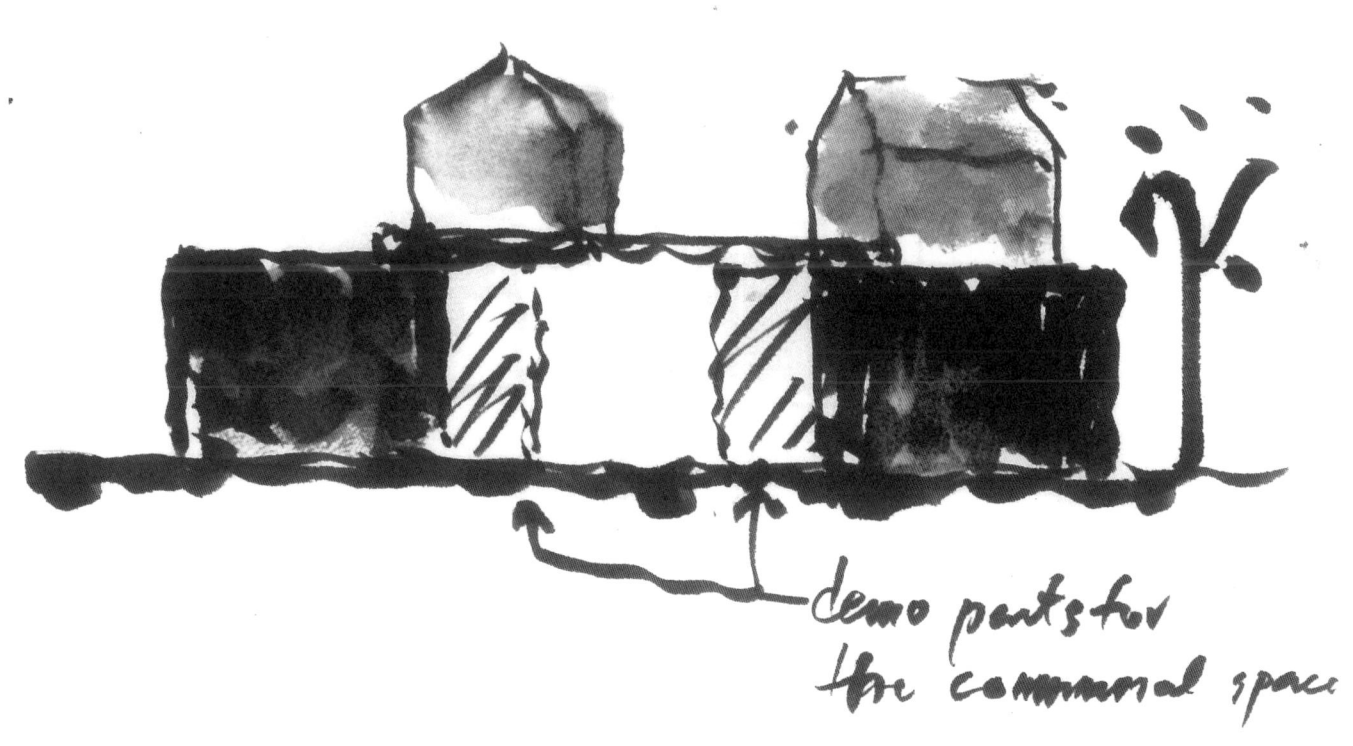

demo parts for
the communal space

Four Piece Housing

This site is located in Mangmi-dong, Busan, within a small town characterized by rows of abandoned factories and aged houses. Project F1963, a regeneration project focused on the abandoned factories that exist in this area, was widely acclaimed for its achievements, invigorating the previously quiet, fading Mangmi-dong, and drawing visitors to the area. However, residents of this area are still prevented from occupying high-quality personal spaces due to the neglected residential spaces and deteriorating public facilities. These public places not only were unused but had been abandoned because they are simply poorly maintained and unattractive. In any urban regeneration project, it is easy to underscore a sense of "publicness" and to focus on the construction of new public places. New buildings do not necessarily embed sustainable values. In order to foster new sustainable values, we believe that one must be informed by the existing urban fabric and its buildings instead of grafting the same kind of new buildings into any given context. As an example of a place that could be used by local residents and serve as a public stronghold, we selected the company housing building built for the employees of the (former) Goryeo Steel, right across from the F1963 building.

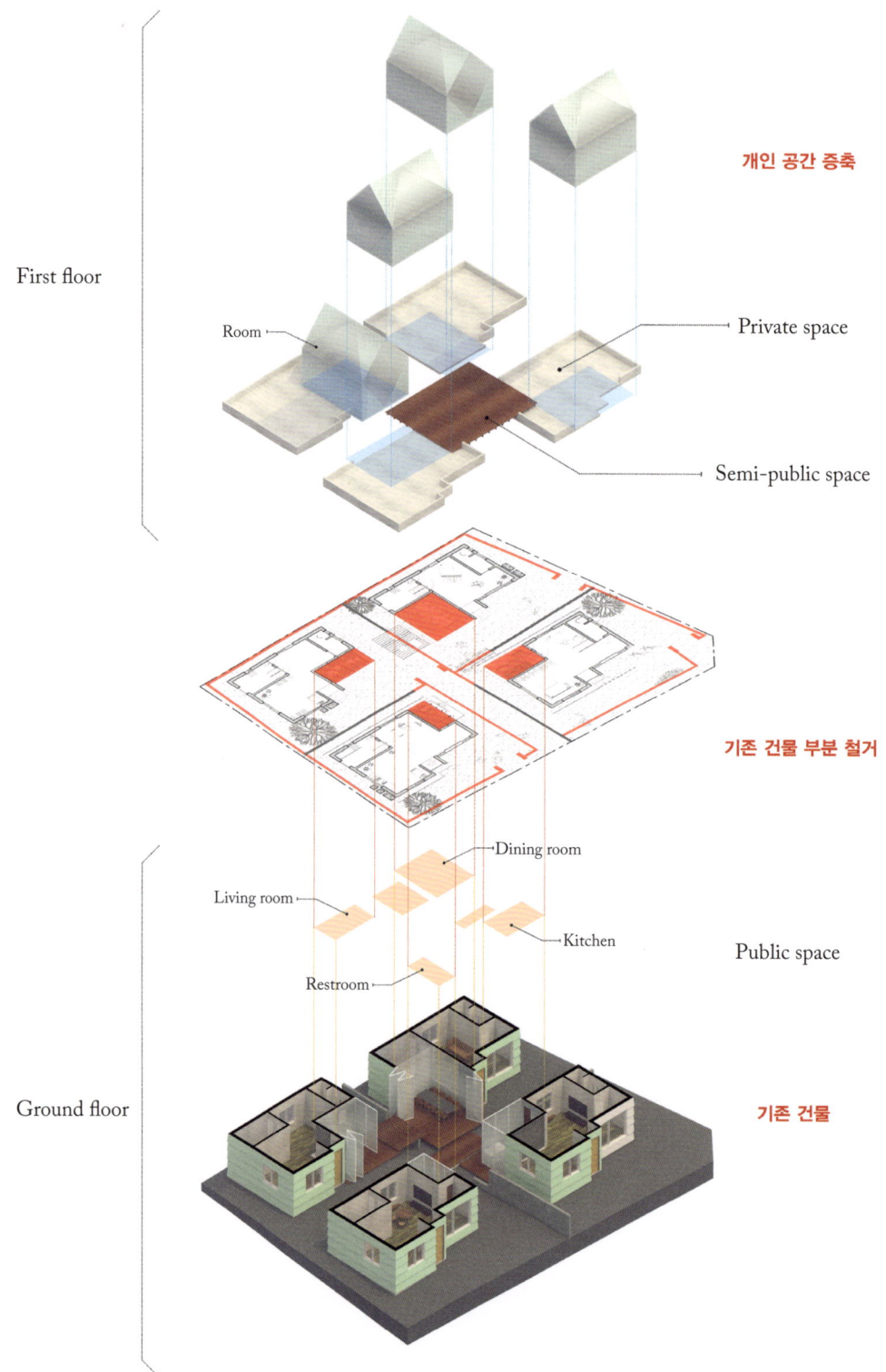

Four Piece Housing

Four Piece Housing

This complex is surrounded by crude cement block fences and consists of a total of four buildings. All four houses had the same form, and separate fences between small parcels were creating ambiguous exterior spaces. The structure, one which appeared to emerge as if from the past, demonstrates the conditions blighting a declining Mangmi-dong. As with the furnace used in the past within a *hanok* (a traditional fourteenth-century-style Korean house), there is a small difference in levels between the living room and the kitchen which makes it inconvenient to move around with ease. A small corridor in the shape of a porch known as *toenmaru* served as a passage connecting the rooms, but it was insufficient to be considered another space of occupation. If we could tear down the fences and give the space proper functions tailored to the rhythms of contemporary lives, we believed that this could become a space of regeneration with the potential to express new values.

However, it looked as if it was going to be difficult to maintain the existing scale; if the entire building was to be redeveloped as a space intended for the public, there would be more concerns and restrictions imposed upon its operations and programs. If we could expand its scale and devise some spaces that could be used by artists or writers, we hoped that some spaces would be able to readily reflect the individuality of their users. In order to place these private spaces for artists and public spaces for local residents, it was important to clearly separate the purposes of and characteristics of each floor. The ground floor was redesigned to be used as an exhibition hall or public space so that artists, as well as local residents, could exhibit or congregate within its walls whenever necessary. The tin-roofed first floor, which was designed to adopt a very lightweight structure like folding a paper, would be where the private spaces for artists are located. The ground and first floors are intuitively separated through established contrasts between different physical properties.

Four Piece Housing

The connection to the city was completely blocked by the fences, and those fences made each building stand independently like an island, blocking each other. In order to employ all spaces freely and flexibly all of the fences had to be demolished, but we understood that removing the fences was not the only solution required. We were able to remove some of the fences, to leave their trace behind, and then cut some of these repurposed pieces to the height required to be used as chairs or tables.

Four Piece Housing remains a proposal as opposed to finding realization as an actual project. Nevertheless, we believe it could be applied to number of places of a similar urban structure to Mangmi-dong. If a system, which daringly provides lower levels or parts of existing buildings with new space while ensuring the autonomy of private spaces, is applied to an area for urban regeneration, it will result in not only the regeneration of a single building but also the strengthening of the values of the surrounding city. As time gradually advances and the members within each household becomes smaller, it is becoming increasingly difficult to form a community as before. If we can allocate spaces for shared use alongside those secured for personal space, cultural solidarity will be fortified between different households and we will encourage a spirit of participation.

SEOMI FURNITURE GALLERY

Reinterpreting the historic fabric with visual communication, experimentation, and an artful plate arrangement

Seoul, Korea | 2003

New/Old on the Antiform
existing house lifted by the
conc. tilt ground

Seomi Furniture Gallery

Based in Cheongdam, Gangnam, Seoul, this is an experimental gallery for young artists (sectioned out in several lots, with two more lots in Jae-dong, Jongno, Seoul). The site is located in a historic area that has typically prioritized *hanok* (a traditional fourteenth-century-style Korean house) construction. Our original design responded to a governing development principle in the urban planning regulations, which indicated that the existing building must be demolished, the four lots must be combined, and the building must be built vertically. Of the buildings remaining on the site, it was deemed necessary to remove the sections of the *hanok* that had been destroyed by a previous fire, including the parts where the original structure had become indiscernible, while those of triangular and atypical shapes were to be left intact as part of the main gallery entry. The remaining facilities could be placed underground, including the exhibition hall. The client, who currently runs a gallery and is well versed in contemporary art and the Korean art scene, happily agreed to this proposal, with a modification that saw the café be located on the ground floor.

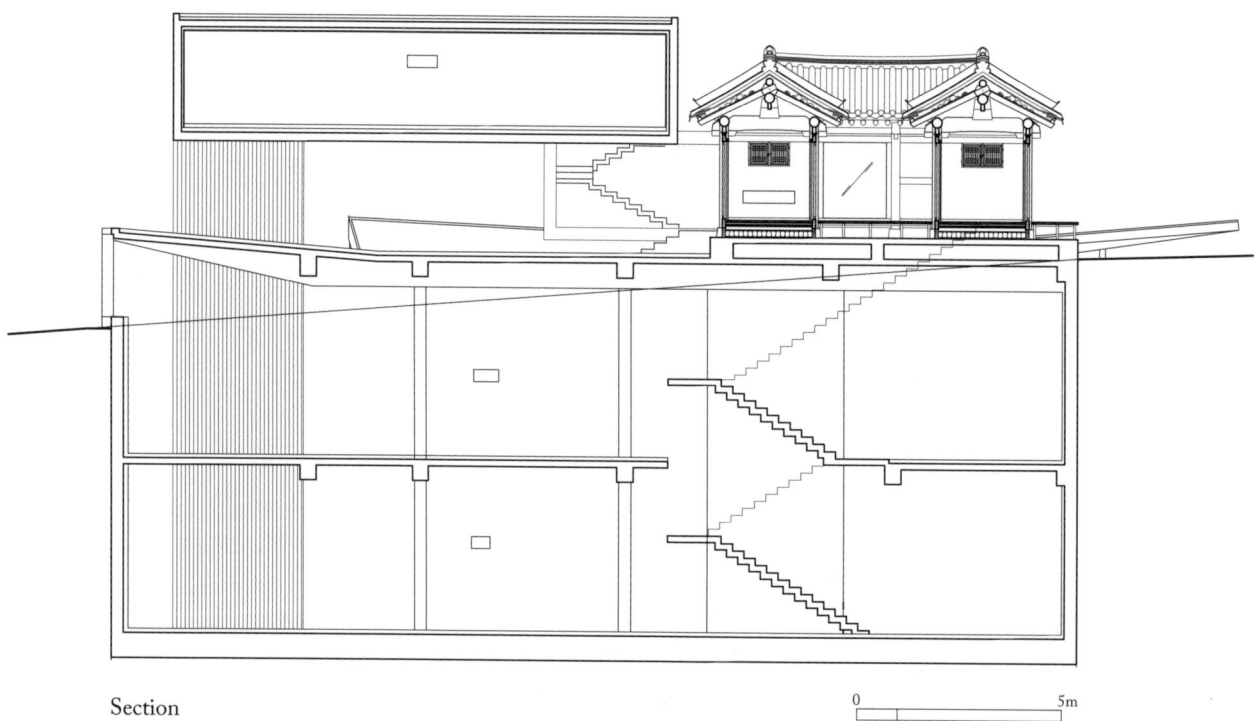

Section

0　　5m

Seomi Furniture Gallery

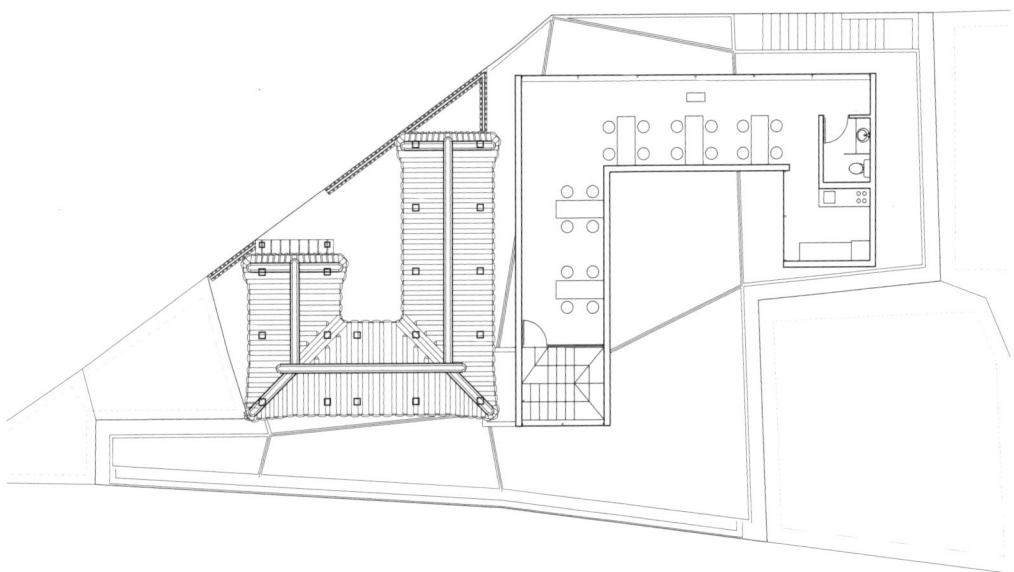

First-floor plan

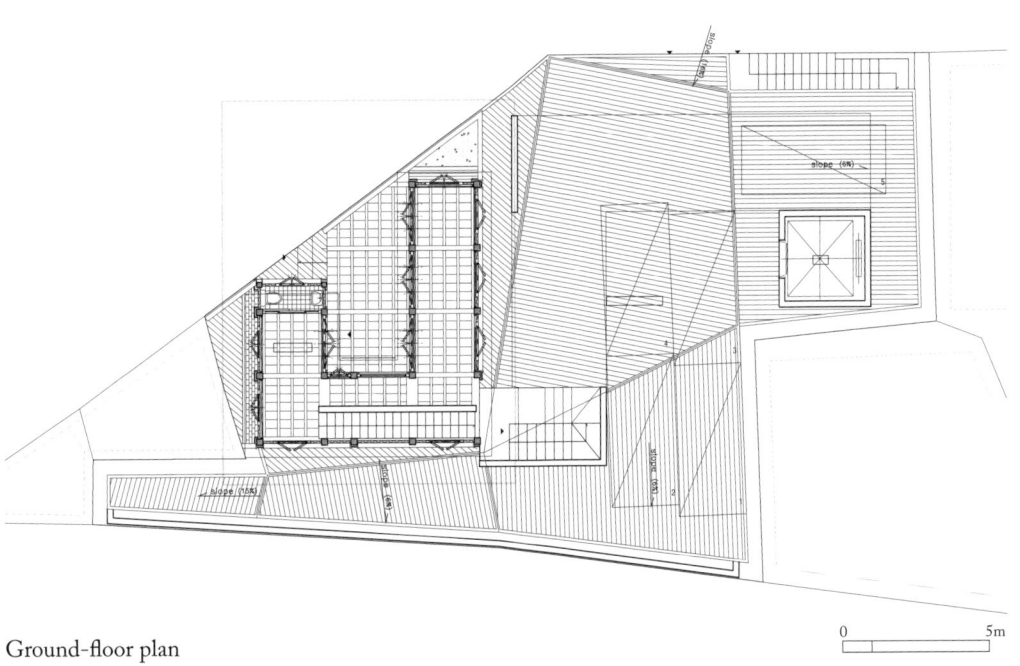

Ground-floor plan

Interpreting the atypical shape of this site to be a single artificial plate, we lifted the rest of the plates along the boundary of the road by a slight degree except for those on the access route to the *hanok*. This allowed natural light to enter the underground exhibition hall, permitting visual communication with the 39-foot-wide (12-meter-wide) road to Seomi Gallery across vacant terrain, while also preventing the more intrusive gazes of the many visitors passing by this historic tourist destination. The 355-square-foot (33-square-meter) *hanok*, left on the artificial site, was reinterpreted based on this design. The reception area, granted significance as the main entrance to the building, also connects the underground exhibition hall to the café aboveground. In this way, as a wide, open plate, the ground floor was proposed as a place in which sculpture and furniture could be displayed, welcoming visitors to the area to pause, rest, and take in some of the installations.

BCHO PARTNERS

BCHO Partners is an architectural office run by Byoung Cho and three associate partners. The office has a workforce of about forty people. It was founded in Seoul, Korea in 1994 as a design-build office with a focus on architecture with simple structures and a strong regard for the natural environment. The design team has through the years worked in close relationship with contractors and multiple fabrication specialists in various disciplines, including stonemasons, product designers, woodworkers, potters, and engineers. The firm has also established multiple professional collaborations throughout the world, especially in North and South America.

The design strategy of BCHO Partners is that buildings, furniture, and art are made—not created. Each architectural project encompasses various scales and programs. Projects explore the phenomenon of light and space, fabrication and construction, recycling and reusing, and a broad range of aspects of sustainability (social, cultural, and physical), which uses the power of creative energy sources to reduce the demand for grid energy.

Over the years, BCHO has experimented widely with the properties embedded in the Korean design tradition, and the understanding of the phenomena of *mahk* (a Korean concept of a design being imperfect and rough) and *bium* (emptiness) is integrated into the design process as an architectural language. The firm continues to initiate numerous forums, exhibitions, and publications that probe the roots of these phenomena and explore the possibilities of *mahk* and *bium* in a contemporary context.

Byoung Cho

Ji-hyun Lee

Ja-yoon Yoon

Kyung-jin Hong

PARTNER PROFILES

Byoung Cho

Principal Partner and Founding Architect of BCHO Partners

Byoung Cho studied the bachelor's program at Montana State University in 1986 and took his master's degree at Harvard University in 1991, with an Exchange Program at ETH Zürich. He has been associated with various universities as a professor and guest professor, including Aarhus School of Architecture, Universitat Kaiserslautern, Yonsei University, Hanyang University, University of Hawaii, and Harvard University.

He has received several distinctions and acknowledgments for his works, including awards from the Korean Institute of Architects (KIA) as well as Cri-Arc, and the American Institute of Architecture (AIA) Honor Award in the Montana Chapter and the Northwest Pacific Region.

Ji-hyun Lee

Partner, Principal Architect, Licensed Architect in Milan, Italy

Ji-hyun Lee graduated in Industrial Design from KAIST, and Architecture and Urban Planning from Politecnico di Milano, in Italy. She worked for Mario Bellini Architects in Milan, where she was exposed to Italian renewal and regeneration contexts in architecture. She then worked for HOK in Hong Kong, China, gaining experience in various international large-scale projects.

She joined BCHO Partners in 2015, and began her Partnership in 2019. She has recently managed and completed the Hyundai Global Learning Center project in Cheonan, which earned the Korean Institute of Architects' award. She is currently overseeing the Visang Headquarters project in Gwacheon, and Seocho Residential Complex project in Seoul, exploring the new typologies in the cityscape through which she tries to recuperate the urban forces that have been ignored in the contemporary Asian cities, while blurring the boundary of the urban/nature dichotomy.

Ja-yoon Yoon

Partner, Principal Architect, Licensed Architect in Korea

Ja-yoon Yoon received her Bachelor of Architecture at Korea University and her Masters of Interior Design at the Royal College of Art in London, United Kingdom. She has participated in various scales of exhibition, most notably with her winning proposal for a pop-up bar at the 2014 May Design Series, London, United Kingdom, and the installation of the Traveling Cinema, and the 2012 Beijing Design Week.

She joined BCHO Partners in 2015 and began her practice as a Partner in 2019. She oversaw the CGV Warehouse Renovation project that investigated the potential of architecture in the renewal of the Incheon Port. In 2016, she taught the fifth-year Architecture Studio, titled "Material Investigations" at the University of Hawaii.

Currently, Ja-yoon is in charge of various projects, including the Hyundai Motors Design Center Renovation, Pyeongchang Farming Village, and the AYU25 Botanical Café. These projects actively study the relationship between architecture, nature, and geographical features and explore the architectural possibilities of creating a "new socio-cultural landscape" (or "socio-culturally sustainable environment").

Kyung-jin Hong

Partner, Principal Architect, Licensed Architect in Korea

Kyung-jin Hong graduated from Ewha Womans University, where she studied architecture and art history. She received her Masters of Architecture at the University of Michigan in the United States. She has built her career in the area of architecture, interior design, and urban projects, and researched various building types across different scales. She was a co-tutor for the "Arts and Crafts" Seoul Studio at the University of Hawaii in 2014 and taught the architecture studio at Hoseo University between 2018 and 2020.

She has worked for BCHO Partners since 2013 and is currently working as a partner of BCHO. Her major projects include Gwangju Memorial, Taejun Park Memorial (Pusan), and Lotte Museum of Art.

Currently, she is overseeing the Seonneung Terrace Hotel and Housing project, focusing on how to weave urban and natural elements of the site into architecture so that it becomes a new stimulus in the existing cityscape.

BCHO STAFF

 **Shinah Lee**
Principal Architect

 **Seungjae Yi**
Project Architect

 **Donguk Choi**
Project Architect

 **Yunseok Jeong**
Project Architect

 **Jinwoo Lee**
Project Architect

 **Jiyeon Yoo**
Project Architect

 **Sookwan Ahn**
Project Architect

 **Sungmin Park**
Project Architect

 **Bokyoung Kim**
Assistant Project Architect

 **Chihoon Lee**
Assistant Project Architect

 **Mingyun Kim**
Assistant Project Architect

 **Seoyoung Park**
Assistant Project Architect

 **Yonghyun Ahn**
Designer

 **Jaekwang Baek**
Junior Designer

 **Yoomin Lee**
Junior Designer

 **Bethel Yoon**
Junior Designer

 **Miju Kim**
Junior Designer

 **Chanyong Lee**
Junior Designer

 **Wooseok Choi**
Junior Designer

 **Jiwoun Lim**
Junior Designer

 **Taewoong Hur**
Junior Designer

 **Youngung Kim**
Junior Designer

 **Jiung Yoo**
Junior Designer

 **Yeowool Noh**
Office Manager

ADVISORY PARTNERS

Eui-Young Chun
Yongsung Chun
Changsuk Ha
Choongsun Lee

Published in Australia in 2022 by
The Images Publishing Group Pty Ltd
ABN 89 059 734 431

Melbourne
6 Bastow Place
Mulgrave, Victoria 3170
Australia
Tel: +61 3 9561 5544

New York
6 West 18th Street 4B
New York, NY 10011
United States
Tel: +1 212 645 1111

Shanghai
6F, Building C, 838 Guangji Road
Hongkou District, Shanghai 200434
China
Tel: +86 021 31260822

Offices
books@imagespublishing.com
www.imagespublishing.com

Copyright © The Images Publishing Group Pty Ltd 2022
The Images Publishing Group Reference Number: 1600

All photography, sketches, plans, and diagrams are supplied courtesy of BCHO Partners.

All rights reserved. Apart from any fair dealing for the purposes of private study, research, criticism or review as permitted under the Copyright Act, no part of this publication may be reproduced, stored in a retrieval system or transmitted in any form by any means, electronic, mechanical, photocopying, recording or otherwise, without the written permission of the publisher.

 A catalogue record for this book is available from the National Library of Australia

Title: Imagining: The Choreography of Land and Architecture // Byoung Cho (BCHO Partners)
ISBN: 9781864709070

This title was commissioned in IMAGES' Melbourne office and produced as follows:
Editorial Georgia (Gina) Tsarouhas, Jeanette Wall *Graphic design* Ryan Marshall
Production Nicole Boehringer

Printed by Artron, China, on 160g Da Dong Woodfree FSC® paper

IMAGES has included on its website a page for special notices in relation to this and its other publications. Please visit www.imagespublishing.com

Every effort has been made to trace the original source of copyright material contained in this book. The publishers would be pleased to hear from copyright holders to rectify any errors or omissions.

The information, illustrations, and photographs in this publication have been prepared and supplied by BCHO Partners (formerly BCHO Architects Associates). While all reasonable efforts have been made to ensure accuracy, the publishers do not, under any circumstances, accept responsibility for errors, omissions and representations express or implied.